Involuntary Resettlement

World Bank Series on Evaluation and Development
Robert Picciotto, Series Editor

Evaluation and Development: The Institutional Dimension,
edited by Robert Picciotto and Eduardo Wiesner

Involuntary Resettlement: Comparative Perspectives,
edited by Robert Picciotto, Warren van Wicklin,
and Edward Rice

Involuntary Resettlement
Comparative Perspectives

World Bank Series on
Evaluation and Development
Volume 2

Robert Picciotto, Warren van Wicklin, and Edward Rice
editors

Transaction Publishers
New Brunswick (U.S.A.) and London (U.K.)

This book is printed on acid-free paper that meets the American National Standard for Permanence of Paper for Printed Library Materials.

Library of Congress Catalog Number: 99-087303
ISBN: 0-7658-0018-7 (cloth); 0-7658-0683-5 (paper)
Printed in the United States of America

Library of Congress Cataloging-in-Publication Data

Involuntary resettlement : comparative perspectives / edited by Robert
Picciotto, Warren van Wicklin and Edward Rice.
       p. cm.—(World Bank series on evaluation and development ; v. 2)
       "Published for The World Bank."
       Includes index.
       ISBN 0-7658-0018-7 (cloth : alk. paper) — ISBN 0-7658-0683-5
(pbk. : alk. paper)
           1. Water resources development—Developing countries—Case studies. 2. Land settlement—Developing countries—Case studies. 3. Forced migration—Developing countries—Case studies
I. Picciotto, Robert. II. Wicklin, Warren van. III. Rice, Edward
IV. Series.

HD1702.I58 2000
333.91'009172'4—dc21   99-087303

Contents

List of Tables

List of Maps

Preface

Among development assistance agencies, the World Bank led the way in the 1980s in establishing a resettlement policy to mitigate the impact of involuntary relocation. During this period the development of a global network of nongovernmental organizations (NGOs) highlighted the failures of past resettlement practices and made resettlement an issue. NGO concerns about resettlement often focused on the predicament of families displaced by dams, overlapping with a broader critique of big dams. Allegations about mishandling of resettlement and blame for damage to the environment are among the challenges faced by the Bank in demonstrating that it is a responsible and caring development agency.

This study selected projects from six countries all appraised well after the resettlement guidelines were first issued and while they were being strengthened. Two projects each were included from India and China, to assess the representativeness of the primary selections from the two countries that dominate the portfolio. Project selection was limited to involuntary resettlement associated with the construction of big dams. While Bank performance in several of these projects was unsatisfactory during the early phases, it improved significantly during project implementation in all cases except Togo. There, although Bank staff believed that an adequate job had already been done, they were wrong. The ten year lag separating the original policy prescriptions and acceptable Bank activity is disappointing.

On assisting borrowers in improving the circumstances of resettlers and their ability to restore their income, one goal of the Bank's resettlement policy, the record is mixed but improving. An encouraging sign is that even in China, with its exemplary policy framework, Bank supervision staff made major contributions to successful implementation, especially in helping the resettlement authorities secure crucial budget additions from the central government earlier than would otherwise have been possible.

On assisting borrowers in avoiding unnecessary resettlement operations or reducing the scale of unavoidable displacements, the study found no evidence that the projects did so. The one case where an initial design was radically downsized to avoid displacement was in Thailand, and that decision was made independent of the Bank. In China, the full supply level was dictated by the need to minimize the impact of flooding on Nanping City (but not on the smaller riverside communities). The Bank was not involved in that decision either.

Elsewhere, whatever positive influence the Bank may have had is presumably hidden in preproject files, when initial designs may have been influenced by Bank engineers. It is unlikely that the Bank's resettlement experts were involved at that stage. One major disappointment is in India, where the authorities set the displacement issue aside in their drive to create reservoir capacity before the end of 2000. The Bank, having been unable to persuade the state government to reverse course, closed the loan and credit.

On influencing the resettlement policies of borrowing countries, this study found excellent results. The Bank can take satisfaction from the broad acceptance of its resettlement policy. The gradual move in Indonesia toward more responsible resettlement, at least by the water authority, is the good result of a bad experience. The Indonesians recognize the Bank's influence in promoting that reform. The Bank has indeed provided the "equity compass" that its pioneering expert struggled so hard to sell to a dismissive audience. Yet there is no evidence that attention to resettlement during implementation and supervision has been mainstreamed. Where task managers—usually engineers—were aggressive in supporting the resettlement component, the experience was favorable.

This suggests the obvious: the commitment of task managers is a crucial factor in Bank performance, alongside specialists in resettlement support. For too long the resettlement components were delegated to resettlement experts, and their suggestions were often ignored or watered down. A few of them were criticized for arrogance or poor teamwork, but they may have seen no other way of being heard. As a group, the sociologists, anthropologists, and other professionals on the teams of resettlement experts must be applauded for having persevered in this often frustrating crusade. Much harm could have been avoided by paying more attention to them. Much harm could also have been avoided if the Bank had staffed missions with agriculturalists and other subject matter specialists in the relevant production categories making up the income programs, as it does routinely for voluntary resettlement programs.

The Bank also has not used suitable instruments or displayed enough perseverance to support its policy. It needs to be involved both upstream and downstream of the engineering project cycle. Involuntary resettlement cannot be covered concurrently with the engineering plans. By the time the engineering plans are appraised, the initial plans for resettlement should already be on the table. The orchard seedlings should be ready for planting about the time the project is negotiated. The agencies responsible for implementation of resettlement should have been tested in the field, and government's commitment to follow through confirmed. The Bank must accept responsibility for ensuring that these preliminary conditions are met before the construction program begins. Only later, when the dam is finished, the project is nearing completion, and the Bank prepares to exit, is the most important phase of resettlement about to begin. A different mix of lending and nonlending instruments is needed to extend Bank involvement in both directions. In particular, the new adaptable lending instruments should be used, especially in testing institutional capacity and technical viability. And implementation of loan and credit covenants should be maintained until the loan or credit has been repaid.

The Bank has changed its policies, but compliance remains a massive challenge. Far more than conditionality and paper plans, compliance requires staunch country commitment, appropriate domestic legislation, and adequate enforcement and implementation capacity. The constraint is not the engineering hardware. It is the societal software—the rules of economic and social governance, and the ability of local agencies to get things done. So paper plans must give way to a proven capacity to deliver. These objectives must be communicated clearly to clients and presented as the standards by which the Bank will determine whether resettlement performance is satisfactory. The recommendation will go nowhere, however, unless the Bank improves its own capacity to provide a candid analysis of borrower capacity and commitment—and unless it defines the necessary conditions for a "go/no-go" decision.

Change is unfolding—globally and locally. Technologically, imitation, adaptation, and shared experiences have improved the ways dams are built. In particular, safety standards are now better understood and disseminated. The time has come to promote a similar change process for the human and ecological dimensions of large dam projects. Fact finding is more effective than fault finding. The Bank needs a rigorous, professional, and transparent process for defining the scope, objectives, organization, and financing of follow-up work. The Bank also needs to develop basic guidelines for involvement by governments, the private sector, and NGOs—as well as broader community and public participation, and better information disclosure and dissemination of results.

For the World Bank, developing partnerships is a key element in reaching out to the world of stakeholders prepared to remain involved. However, the Bank does not need to be at the center, at the top, or in the most prominent seat. What is important is that the issues be addressed effectively. The Bank wants to be sure that follow-up actions gradually lead to standards for assessing, planning, building, operating, and financing large dams that are generally accepted by the governments and the people of the developing world and by the external agencies—public, private, and voluntary—with a stake in the development process.

Clearly the Bank needs to trigger real change. Generally accepted standards and best-practice examples should be sought to get results on the ground. Equally, new ways of cooperation must replace the current gridlock of distrust and recrimination. Governments of developed and developing countries will have to be involved far more than they have been so far. The private sector will also have to be a key player in the next steps. Dams will continue to be built—however, if ways are not found out of the current logjam, they will be built at a slower pace than necessary, with great pain and higher human and environmental cost. Instead, a win–win logic is needed, so that the history of dam construction can evolve from confrontation to cooperation—for the benefit of all.

Robert Picciotto
Director-General
Operations Evaluation
The World Bank
October 1999
Washington, D.C.

RESETTLEMENT SITES EVALUATED BY OED

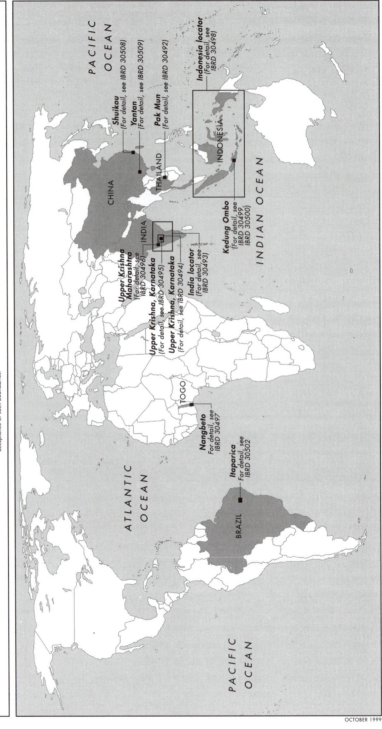

IBRD 30491

PACIFIC
OCEAN

Shuikou
(For detail, see IBRD 30508)

Yantan
(For detail, see IBRD 30509)

Pak Mun
(For detail, see IBRD 30492)

CHINA

THAILAND

Indonesia locator
(For detail, see
IBRD 30498)

INDONESIA

INDIA

Upper Krishna
Maharashtra
(For detail, see
IBRD 30496)

Upper Krishna, Karnataka
(For detail, see IBRD 30495)

Upper Krishna, Karnataka
(For detail, see IBRD 30494)

India locator
(For detail, see IBRD 30493)

Kedung Ombo
(For detail, see
IBRD 30499,
IBRD 30500)

INDIAN OCEAN

TOGO

Nangbeto
For detail, see
IBRD 30497

Itaparica
For detail, see
IBRD 30502

ATLANTIC
OCEAN

BRAZIL

PACIFIC
OCEAN

OCTOBER 1999

1

Overview

For some, large dams symbolize a failed, centralized, technocratic approach to development characterized by waste, bureaucratic bungling, and insensitivity to people and the environment. For others, large dams are almost cathedrals—the supreme creation of an era, conceived with passion by unknown artists and adopted in image, if not in usage, by a whole population. Both myths survive because each contains a grain of truth. Some dams are marvels of human ingenuity. They make deserts bloom. They tame floods. They produce clean energy. They also put nature to work. However, a large dam can also silence a river, destroy a landscape, endanger biodiversity, and uproot whole communities. That is why we continue the search for economic and social solutions that can provide more and better goods and services for all—while sustaining a high-quality environment.

The dilemmas posed by large dams are those of harmonizing development with the environment. At the core of this challenge lies energy—the fuel of economic development. However, energy does not have to mean burning carbon, and dams have a significant role to play in freeing the energy system from carbon consumption. When built on time and on budget, they produce electric power at competitive prices. That power can substitute for power derived from wood, coal, kerosene, and oil—and thus contribute to a cleaner, safer, healthier environment. Hydroelectric power can also reduce the deadly wastes associated with open fire and smoke in homes and workplaces and with the exposure to pneumonia, TB, diphtheria and other airborne disease. It can make refrigeration possible, cutting into waterborne gastrointestinal diseases—another major killer.

Hydroelectric power has other advantages. Rather than requiring foreign exchange for fossil fuels, hydroelectric power is renewable and a domestic resource. More than that, hydroelectric plants are easy to operate and maintain. No wonder, then, that two-thirds of the large dams built in the 1980s were in developing countries. The power market in these countries is growing, and that is where the bulk of unexploited sites reside. According to the World Energy Council, energy production for hydroelectric power will double from 2,000 terawatt hours in 1990 to 4,000 terawatt hours in 2020. This implies a trebling of hydro capacity—still leaving 70 percent of the technically usable potential untapped.

There is thus a strong economic and environmental case for large dams. However, as dams are currently designed, constructed, and implemented, a strong case can also be made against them. The damming of a river can be a cataclysmic event in the life of a riverine ecosystem. The construction of dams in areas that are densely populated, environmentally sensitive, and institutionally weak can be very destructive. Just as in real estate, location matters. Consultation with affected people matters, too, but it's not a panacea. The protection of natural habitats and the resettlement of people displaced by dams call for institutions and implementation capacities that need nurturing over many years, even decades.

The resettlement issues surrounding dam projects are inherently more difficult than those of nondam projects. Construction of dams and their related reservoirs usually requires the acquisition of large, consolidated pieces of land. Withdrawing this land from production eliminates the main means of livelihood for its owners, and that land often cannot be easily replaced nearby. Dams are in rural areas where incomes are more difficult to restore, not least because the dams inundate fertile river valleys, pushing people into less fertile uplands, which call for new skills to manage.

The purpose of this study is not to ascertain the extent of problems with resettlement. Instead, it is to illuminate the range of experience in recently completed resettlement operations to determine what works well and what does not— and to suggest means of improving performance.

Despite the debacles and disappointments, there have been some surprisingly good outcomes. The China projects show what can be done to make resettlement work when the executing agencies are prepared to do so with the tools and opportunities available—and when the Bank can protect and reinforce the commitment by government. What China does, others can do as well. In Thailand and Indonesia, resettlers were picked up and carried along by tidal changes in the regional economy. The outcomes suggest that planners can be more aggressive in designing compensation packages linked to non-land-based diversification strategies to put displaced people back to work.

Most Projects Selected for the Study Have Greater Resettlement Problems than Typical Bank-Assisted Projects with Dams

The projects selected for this study range widely in size (map IBRD 30491). On average they displace about four times as many people as other World Bank projects with dams. The dams, on average, were not significantly more expensive or larger in reservoir surface area, but they were in more densely populated areas. This study also reflects the roughly even split between dams built for hydropower and those built for irrigation, but it does not include dams built primarily for drinking-water supply or transportation.

The projects selected have generally had greater resettlement problems than most Bank-assisted projects. Three are among the most controversial in the Bank's entire portfolio. A higher percentage of the case-study projects had resettlement problems than the portfolio as a whole, largely because more recently approved projects have generally had fewer problems. The selected projects are described below.

India—Upper Krishna

The Krishna River is one of the three main rivers of the Indian subcontinent, originating in the Western Ghats, in the State of Maharashtra, and flowing east through the States of Karnataka and Andhra Pradesh before emptying into the Bay of Bengal. The study examined resettlement at four dams, two in each state. In Karnataka, the Narayanpur reservoir was not completely filled until 1996. The dam at Almatti is still not finished, and resettlement is in the early stages. Narayanpur displaced 5,100 households; Almatti is expected to displace 33,000 households, and the construction of canals, drains, and roads will displace another 2,600 households. The total of 40,000 households, or about 240,000 people, is the largest resettlement operation in the Bank's history. This does not include another 150,000 to 200,000 people who will be displaced when Almatti is raised to its ultimate height.

The two dams in Maharashtra, Dhom and Kanher, are on the upper reaches of the Krishna. They are each about one-fifth the size of Narayanpur. Dhom displaced 3,390 families and Kanher displaced 3,860 families, for a total of about 40,000 people. The Dhom displacees had ten more years to get established, and because they moved into the functioning, upper reaches of the irrigation command, they are generally doing better than the Kanher displacees, most of whom are in the lower reaches of the command, where property disputes have delayed construction of irrigation canals up to ten years. Some of these people have already have been waiting up to 17 years for irrigation they were promised in 1980.

China—Shuikou and Yantan

These two Chinese dams, both in narrow valleys surrounded by hills, have reservoirs about 100 kilometers long. At Shuikou, relocation began in 1988, but almost 70 percent of the 67,200 people evacuated from the valley floor were moved between 1990 and 1992. Another 17,200 in Nanping City, at the upstream end of the reservoir, had to be moved to make way for the construction of embankments to protect the downtown area and avoid the need for relocating more of Nanping's nearly 200,000 inhabitants. The full supply level of the reservoir was set below the optimal economic level precisely to avoid massive displacement in the city. The resettlers were housed in ten large apartment buildings constructed on sites scattered through the city, including immediately behind the embankments. This meant that people could continue their previous jobs. All relocation was completed by the end of 1992, and the reservoir was filled in 1993.

At Yantan, as at Shuikou, the objective was to move people short distances, and into comparable occupations. Again, it started with a land-based strategy. Yantan has a harsher topology, and plowable land is even scarcer than at Shuikou. Yantan is much farther from any large cities and farther still from the booming coastal economy. By March 1992, 43,200 people had moved, with an additional 19,200 affected. By March 1997, jobs had been arranged for 17,000 people out of a labor force of 25,000. In 1992, the agency relocated 3,600 people—with 1,000 arranged jobs—to two former state sugar farms near Guangxi Province's own developing coastal center at Beihai. In 1997, 11,500 more people had to move— with 3,000 arranged jobs—to another government farm in Binyang in central Guangxi.

Thailand—Pak Mun

Pak Mun is in northeast Thailand, on the lower reaches of the Mun River, 5.5 kilometers above its confluence with the Mekong, which forms the border between Thailand and Laos. The power company that built the dam changed the design by lowering the dam height five meters, which reduced power benefits by one-third, more than halved the reservoir length and surface area, and reduced the number of inundated families from 4,000 to 240. Families whose houses would be within 30 meters of the reservoir—excessively isolated by the reservoir, or inconvenienced by dam construction—were offered compensation packages equal to those whose houses would be inundated. As a result, another 670 households were resettled in addition to the original 240. By May 1993, only two households had not consented to land acquisition. The relocation was extraordinarily easy. Some households literally moved across the street. Most families moved less than a kilometer, many opting to move from riverside clusters to linear alignments along the significantly improved trunk road paralleling the left bank of the river.

Brazil—Itaparica

The damming of northeast Brazil's São Francisco River at Itaparica began in 1979 and was completed in 1988, creating a reservoir 149 kilometers long with a surface area of 840 square kilometers. It displaced 3,500 urban, 1,000 pararural (people who moved to towns but retained rights to irrigated lots), and 4,900 rural families (including 400 families displaced by the new irrigation works). Another 1,000 families received cash compensation and left the area.

Stage I—the construction of facilities and transfer of families into four new towns and 127 *agrovilas* (new villages)—ranks among the quickest and most successful of any large relocation operation. Private contractors worked under intense pressure throughout 1987 and the first half of 1988 to complete the works. Most families were still moving when the sluice gates at the dam were closed in February 1988, but ongoing relocation activities could keep up with the rising water and the residents were not at risk. The resettlers received much better houses (in most cases) with water and electric connections.

Stage II called for the provision of irrigation water through pressurized pipes to sprinkler systems installed on 5,900 demarcated lots ranging from 1.5 to 6.0 hectares, and totaling 20,500 hectares. Stage II is still far from complete nine years after resettlers moved to the *agrovilas* and eight years after the deadline by which they had been assured all the schemes would be brought into production. By June 1997, 2,300 lots totaling 8,000 hectares, or 40 percent of the total, were receiving water. Another 1,800 lots and 6,600 hectares, about 30 percent of the total, were expected to be fully operational by the end of 1998. The other 1,800 lots, the final 30 percent, were still "under study," but these lots have such marginal soils that they may never receive irrigation. Many of the farmers assigned to these lots may be assigned new lots, or may be helped to establish other forms of livelihood.

Indonesia—Kedung Ombo

About 50 kilometers southeast of Semarang, the provincial capital on the north coast of Central Java, the Kedung Ombo dam intersects a river system that once annually restored the fertility of the river valleys and part of the floodplains. The reservoir inundated most of this intensively farmed land. The surrounding Kedung Ombo hills are among the least suitable parts of the province for subsistence agriculture. The original survey found that 75 percent of the 24,000 resettlers indicated that they would join Indonesia's massive transmigration program and resettle to the outer islands. During implementation, however, only 25 percent of the resettlers transmigrated.

The government relaxed its pressure on families to move out of the greenbelt area surrounding the reservoir. (About 600 have stayed.) At stake were 9,000 hectares, perhaps half of its prime cultivable land, and perhaps three-quarters of that available for at least one crop during annual drawdowns of the reservoir. The government also cleared three villages in Forest Department lands to create space for another 700 families. The largest number of resettlers, 2,800 families, accepted the compensation money and resettled themselves. Most settled in the hills above the lake, although many had to find off-farm employment to restore their incomes. Given the rapidly expanding economy of Central Java, this was a viable option.

About 1,250 families transmigrated to 17 sites on Sumatra, Kalimantan, and Irian Jaya. The largest cluster, about 310 families, went to Muko Muko in Bengkulu Province on Sumatra. An inexplicable error in site planning placed many on land underlain by a medium to thick strata of peat, an almost impossible soil for irrigation. While the land could be salvaged for tree crops, and possibly even maize or other field crops, the government has stubbornly insisted that the resettlers grow rice. The 86 resettler families transmigrated to an irrigation site on Irian

Jaya are doing reasonably well, and the 193 families relocated to East Kalimantan are doing the best of all with their two hectares of oil palm each.

Togo—Nangbeto

The first hydropower project in Togo, Nangbeto, is on the Mono River, 160 kilometers upstream of the coast and 80 kilometers upstream of where it begins to form the border between Togo and Benin. The reservoir and resettlement areas are entirely within Togo, but the power is shared with Benin, through the binational power company, Communauté Electrique du Bénin. The reservoir displaced 10,600 people. Of this total, 7,600 lost their houses and land and were moved to resettlement zones 30 to 55 kilometers northeast of their former locations. The other 3,000 lost their houses but little of their land. They were moved back a few kilometers from the reservoir and could continue to farm most of their former lands.

The physical relocation went well without any incidents. The 7,600 people moved to the resettlement zones were relocated in two months, after their December 1986 harvest and in time to prepare their fields for spring planting. The power company provided two-room core houses and cash compensation to finish the houses according to individual needs and priorities. The resettlement zone was sparsely populated, the soils were fresh, and land had been easily obtained from host communities. Resettlement villages were provided with boreholes with pumps, and other community infrastructure.

Project Compensation Rates and Schedules Vary but Are Improving in Terms of Fairness and Timeliness

The experience with compensation rates and schedules ranges widely, but the trend appears to be toward improvements in fairness and timeliness. Governments are moving toward broad acceptance of the principle that displaced families should be paid the real value of their lost assets. However, compensation is still a major issue in many projects and progress is slow.

Resettlers did not complain about—and therefore presumably were satisfied with—their compensation for lost houses and trees that were economic assets ("economic" trees). Nangbeto, where people were promised payment for trees but never got it, was an exception. Elsewhere people got what their assets were worth and, in several cases, could keep the salvageable material from the old house without discount or were provided with a new house or the two-room core of a house and compensation or both. One difficulty arose when many families used the funds to build at the same time, causing a shortage of materials and inflating labor as well as material costs. None of the projects compensated at enhanced rates to provide for this. More frequently, a problem arose when families were paid cash in a lump sum long before the deadline for moving, so that the compensation funds were spent on other necessities and were no longer available when the families needed them. That is a scheduling problem, extraordinarily difficult to avoid wherever responsibility for rebuilding is left with displacees who move at the last moment. A solution practiced in some countries was to have installment payments accompany the pace of building. However, this discouraged early movement. These problems usually emerged years after the project authority had agreed with the families about the house and home-yard compensation package. Displacees would grumble belatedly over compensation rates when they were really unhappy about the process.

Controversy over compensation involving payments for lost cultivable land affected three of the projects, but in only one—Kedung Ombo—did the issue blow up. There and at the two sites in India, compensation rates that probably approximated market values when the properties were surveyed were hopelessly inadequate to finance replacement purchases when the displacees entered the land market in large numbers. Payment schedules were also inappropriate, for the same reasons as for house compensation: cash paid as a lump sum too long before the move was spent for other purposes, but tranching discouraged or limited purchases by those who wanted to move early. Adjustments were later made for displacees of the two dams in Karnataka, including an extra grant paid to all families sufficient to help them extend their property marginally. The authorities there have also provided an additional grant for house improvement. However, even though the total compensation in both cases may have been adequate, receiving it in two installments ten years apart is obviously an ineffective, second-best solution.

Of the three projects where land compensation was intended to be invested in land, in two only a small amount was used in this way: six percent at Pak Mun, and 26 percent at Narayanpur. (Data are not available for Kedung Ombo.) At Kedung Ombo, the provincial government never significantly adjusted compensation despite overwhelming evidence that it should, explaining the intensity of the resistance that developed.

At Pak Mun, families in the vicinity of the reservoir—subsequent to compensation and physical relocation of homes and fields on exceedingly generous terms—came back to insist on compensation for the dam's effect on fishing. Residents, regardless of whether their property had been affected, and supported by NGOs, claimed additional compensation for what they asserted to be a decline in the value of the fishery since the reservoir was created (an ongoing research program will test that assertion). The project authority has already made additional payments for fishing losses, but the formula was unsatisfactory and other claimants have appeared in the meantime.

Such claims raise an issue that has troubled many other resettlement programs: the arrival in the reservoir area of pseudo-resettlers claiming project benefits for which they do not qualify. For the cases here, this was not a serious concern. True, there were latecomers to Itaparica hoping to get a free irrigation plot, transmigrants from the districts around Kedung Ombo who falsely claimed to be from the reservoir, and bogus fishermen claiming lost fishing income at Pak

Mun. However, the scale of this deception was nowhere great enough to significantly dilute the packages aimed at genuine displacees.

Land compensation rates were not challenged at Itaparica, where all families were eligible for an irrigated lot proportional in size to owned land that was lost and where the landless were also given small lots. The Maharashtra state government awarded small, irrigated lots to displaced, landless families who elected to resettle in the command areas of those two dams.

Compensation for agricultural land inundated behind big dams is inherently contentious. Large numbers of displaced farmers will not be able to find fields in surrounding hills with comparable fertility and ease of tillage as in the abandoned valley (except for small, scattered plots with inflated prices governments are unwilling to match). Controversy can be expected wherever the policy of "land for nearby land" prevails. Attempts to index compensation rates to land prices will not work in these hills because not enough land is available. Increasing those rates will only provide resettlers with more money to purchase the same amount of land, leading to an inflationary spiral. So the sense of having given up something better will forever shape dam displacees' attitudes.

One generic category of assets rarely compensated (the Pak Mun fishery is the only example) is customary claims on common property: loss of access to flooded forests and other productive public lands. Although the surveys did not inquire specifically into this subject, it occasionally came up in discussions about overall satisfaction with the move. The projects in China and Togo are in a different category. There, all the inundated land—cultivated, fallow, and forest—belonged to the community, not to individuals, so the project authorities negotiated the compensation with village leaders—an arrangement that gave no cause for complaint.

The Relocation Record Is Uneven but Mostly Satisfactory

The record with relocation—the individual or collective movement of people up and out of the reservoir boundaries—was uneven but on the whole satisfactory. The tempo of relocation is generally driven by the advancing water: as in developed countries, families stay in the valleys as long as they can. In only one case—at the Almatti dam in Karnataka in 1996 and 1997—did the water catch the people before the new sites were ready to receive them, so that emergency action had to be taken, including boats and helicopters, to evacuate a large number of those who were ousted. When this happens, it is a clear sign that the construction schedule for the dam was not synchronized with that for resettlement, and the dam took priority. Apparently, the authorities gambled that an exceptional flood would not occur before all the people were out—and lost the bet. There is, however, no excuse for losing this kind of bet twice. Flooding people out of their homes should never be accepted as the method of relocation.

Elsewhere, relocation kept pace with the water. Kedung Ombo appeared to be heading toward disaster, but the dissident families could have moved faster and the few that got caught had declined government transport out. Most of the dissidents moved with the water, building temporary shelters as they went. When the water stopped rising, many of them stopped moving too, settling in a restricted area zoned as a greenbelt and later securing government permission to stay.

In the two cases where project authorities were responsible for constructing new housing, performance was very good. At Itaparica performance was excellent: four new towns and 127 *agrovilas* were established, fully equipped, within a year—without delaying the dam and just in time to avoid the water. At Nangbeto, the core houses in the new settlements were ready before the people were forced to shift. In the other cases, the authorities were responsible for constructing roads and the rest of the community infrastructure needed to prepare for housebuilding by the displacees. Here also, performance was satisfactory. At the two dams in China, the best example of this activity, government first leveled the terraces and created space—and built the infrastructure—for the new towns and villages. The families (except for the incapacitated) then built their homes on lots assigned by lottery. After some delays, the construction and transfer were carried out expeditiously.

Pak Mun again is in a class by itself. The Electricity Generating Authority of Thailand (EGAT) financed the relocation of four times as many houses as were required, and almost all of those 1,000 moves were short distance and accomplished easily. It financed the moves of families that wanted to move away from the noise, dust, and other disturbances of dam construction, even though their homes were not threatened. EGAT also financed other families that would have ended up in isolated positions or closer than they wanted to be to the river. The agency also accompanied the movement of houses by building earthworks to preserve some lakeside properties (mainly houseplots) that would have otherwise been submerged, and by building schools, clinics, temples, and roads. Pak Mun excels in both compensation and relocation.

The Income Restoration Record Is Unsatisfactory

Critics project a grim picture of the impact of dams on the incomes of involuntary resettlers: impoverishment and marginalization. The World Bank acknowledges that the record on restoring—let alone improving—incomes has been unsatisfactory. In a 1993 report, it claimed that average households in two of the four case studies had improved their position, but in one of these (Khao Laem, in Thailand) the improvement was attributable to favorable changes in the economy rather than induced by the project, and in the other (Krishna, in Maharashtra) the sample was later shown to be biased. A follow-up visit to Maharashtra in 1997 revealed that a larger number of displacees had probably suffered income losses. Other recent Bank reports, while not projecting an image of "impoverishment," concede that successful interventions are in the minority.

In three of the case studies, regional growth and job creation buffered the

impact of displacement and greatly facilitated the restructuring of resettler production systems. In none of the three cases—Shuikou, Pak Mun, and Kedung
Ombo—did resettlement planning anticipate the vitality of the regional economy.
The Chinese authorities at Shuikou were already well ahead of the other countries in building into the project plan alternative employment based on local jobs.
However, when they later discerned the additional possibilities introduced by
regional growth, they were quick to jump in that direction. At Pak Mun, the
negative impact of the dam on employment and incomes was minimal, because
the households in that area had already started moving away from cropping—and
because the slightly expanded river did not inundate much of the villages' farm
land. The booming Thai economy lifted the Northeast as well and protected the
people along the river above the Pak Mun dam from most of the adverse effects.
At Kedung Ombo, the rapid developments throughout Java provided timely relief
to a situation that might otherwise have become untenable.

In each of these three cases, off-farm employment opportunities gave jobs to
heads of households and younger family members, replacing the components of
farm income lost to the flood. Income levels were restored and increased above
predam levels at least for most of the displaced families that resettled locally.
That finding is no surprise for anyone familiar with Shuikou—or with Pak Mun
(and not distracted by the campaign against the dam). However, it *is* a surprise
for anyone who has followed the written record of protest at Kedung Ombo.

The diversification of household income streams and economies, and the resulting increase in the share of nonfarm earnings from live-at-home members and
migrant remittances, is not restricted to resettlers. However, it allows them to
escape a possible poverty trap waiting for them in the hills above the lake. Three
other cases reflect similar shifts in income sources, although Yantan—a more
remote location than Shuikou and unable as yet to attract the foreign and local
investments in town and village industries that have invaded Shuikou—local
nonfarm employment is growing, albeit slowly. The authorities, however, are
taking a different route to diversification, promoting the organized transfer of the
poorest-endowed villages of displacees to subdivided large-scale farms in other
districts, including two sugar estates near the coast. At the two project sites in
India, male family members are drifting off in increasing numbers to jobs in the
city—from the Krishna River dams in Maharashtra to Pune and Mumbai (Bombay),
and from the Krishna River dams in Karnataka to Goa and Bangalore. Remittances from even one member, with a low-paid industrial job in Mumbai, can
have a substantial impact on a family's cash holdings.

At the other two projects, Nangbeto and Itaparica, no shift toward a more
diversified income pattern is discernible. For Nangbeto this is expected, since
there has been little movement off the farms (except for minor local trading) and
the Togolese economy was in decline from 1990 to 1995. For Itaparica it is
expected, because outmigration to the cities is a tradition of the drylands of
northeast Brazil. However, the migrants that leave do not send money home, and
thus do not reinforce the household economies as they do in Asia.

Itaparica is atypical in all respects. The project was limited to resettlement, and irrigator income was the prime objective. However, the irrigation systems are incomplete. Marketing problems have depressed incomes on the subschemes that have started production. In addition, all rural families—whether on irrigated lots or waiting for irrigation—receive a monthly maintenance subsidy worth more than the irrigation income. The families have become so dependent on this subsidy that discussions of its withdrawal trigger bitter protests. Despite having the highest incomes (for irrigating families), Itaparica suffers from the greatest measure of discontent and threat of violence.

Where it is not practical to provide displacees with irrigated lots next to the lake or below the dam, the land-for-nearby-land strategy has little applicability to reservoir resettlement, at least in already crowded regions. Land-for-land without the "nearby" tag is practical where transmigration is feasible. However, in crowded regions with no transmigration alternatives, the primary objective should be to encourage diversification.

As a first step, this strategy could concentrate on alternative production opportunities in agriculture. Here, the Chinese experience is valuable, because the authorities at Shuikou and Yantan tried first to exploit niche activities on the land or water that remained underdeveloped yet might thrive on the resources left after the reservoir filled. These included orchards on terraced slopes; bamboo and tea on the steeper slopes; forestry on the steepest slopes; goats in the drier hills; integrated fish, duck, and hog farms near the lake; oyster beds and fish cages in the lake; and pigs and mushrooms in confined spaces next to the houses. The intensity of this broad attack on available resources is remarkable; none of the other countries came close to this. Fish cages at Kedung Ombo might have been an exception, but they have not been popular. The fact that nothing was organized for the families living in the *agrovilas* at Itaparica while they were waiting for water—and even though they had been paid the subsidy—is inexcusable.

Therefore, when authorities found the agricultural-based employment strategy insufficient to absorb the displaced workers, they looked outside agriculture for a second generation of employment opportunities to accommodate the full work force. Shuikou moved into local industry; Yantan transferred the excess population out. Most impressively, at Shuikou, when the new enterprises failed, as many have done, the town and village authorities worked with the entrepreneurs to restructure the business and bring it back to profitability, a follow-through to a third-generation strategy.

What best explains China's unique performance is its system of government—and vision. The provincial authorities there look upon a resettlement recovery program as an *opportunity* rather than a *burden* (an unavoidable cost of the dam). "Favorable policy and planning frameworks, and local institutions that have high stakes in the continuing productivity of their citizens, combine to produce resettlement operations with very high ratings."[1]

Some of that grander vision of opportunities for development accompanied the planning stages for Itaparica, but the vision dimmed as the plans for irrigation gelled and then disappeared during implementation. Another disappointment in income recovery performance is that the special income strategies promoted in two countries to reinforce the faltering land-for-land programs—strategies conceived and implemented long after appraisal—have both been ineffective. These include the Resettlement and Reservoir Development Program at Kedung Ombo and the more recent income-generating schemes in both states in India.

Social Infrastructure and Services Are the Most Successful Components of Projects

Social infrastructure and services is the part of the resettlement program that usually receives the best ratings. A 1993 Bank study reports that "social infrastructure services—water, health, education, electricity, access roads—were, in general, much better in all projects than before resettlement."[2] The cases here suggest that the conclusion needs more careful phrasing, and that the qualifier "much" should be removed. A distinction should be drawn between the physical infrastructure and the supporting services required to put that infrastructure to best use and maintain it.

For physical infrastructure, improvements are evident everywhere and welcomed by the resettler communities. This is especially true for roads, which have been extended and hard-surfaced, substantially increasing accessibility. Electric and water supply connections to individual homes and community fixtures have been expanded to a large number of households; these facilities are particularly appreciated where none existed before. The number of medical clinics and primary schools has also increased—and to less extent, the proportional equivalent of secondary schools. These improvements also invite favorable remarks from resettlers, with the expansion of educational infrastructure, along with roads, noted most often in interviews.

However, except at the two sites in China, people frequently complain about the operation and maintenance of these structures, particularly about the erratic or poor quality of human services and the material supplies provided. This can be location specific. In the Itaparica *agrovilas* and towns, resettler complaints about inadequate medical services and supplies and provision of sewer systems and sanitation varied by location. More often, the complaints are generic, and indicating a failure of local authorities to operate the services at a level commensurate with the structures built—or to fund adequate upkeep.

Indian and Togolese respondents complained about these shortfalls. Itaparica has had a continuing problem supplying the primary schools with teachers, most of whom are recruited in towns and unhappy living in remote *agrovilas*. In Indonesia, although comments were usually positive, the resettlers in the three government-built villages near the reservoir suffer from inadequate maintenance of the water supply systems, and most transmigrants had to rely on traditional sources of water supply and are not connected to electricity. The most serious failing in the whole study was the inability of the Karnataka government to arrest the spread of malaria around the Narayanpur reservoir despite building clinics. The incidence of infection reached epidemic proportions, increasing from 262 cases in 1991 to 3,990 cases in 1996. All right-bank villages reported deaths in 1996, when the reservoir was at a record level and closer to the resettler villages than ever before.

Another serious failure was at Nangbeto, where a general collapse of the borehole pumps interrupted water supply to the new communities. These project-provided water supply systems attracted the host population to such an extent the pumps were overworked at a time when the project authorities expected the resettlers to take over responsibility for operation and maintenance costs. Most of the pumps are now out of action, and most resettlers are worse off than they were before the dam because they now have to walk farther to get water.

The general problem is that local authorities who must staff and maintain service facilities after the project authorities withdraw are faced with competing demands from nonproject communities. The civil administrators are less likely than the project managers to treat the resettlers as a privileged group. In the new villages at Nangbeto, preferential treatment for the involuntary migrants in the midst of similar communities of hosts and voluntary migrants was not sustainable. The problem shows up in all public services, including agricultural extension. Resettled ex-paddy farmers in Karnataka and Kedung Ombo require expert support to create a dryland cropping system. Their traditional farming skills are ill suited to the new environment. However, the local agricultural service is unable (and usually unwilling) to give them special attention. At Kedung Ombo, the extension agents are trained to concentrate on paddy agriculture, putting most resettlers outside their circuit.

In short, although the social infrastructure in the resettlement communities is invariably lavish compared with that of unaffected communities, the costs of operation and maintenance revert to local administrations that have typically been unable to maintain them at full capacity. Therefore, the continuing success of this relatively good side of the resettlement operation cannot be taken for granted. Greater involvement of the communities is needed for sustainability. All too often, however, resettlement has engendered a sense of dependency on public institutions.

Resettler Satisfaction Varies among Projects

At the two sites in China, clearly positive economic effects have been recorded, and satisfaction levels are high. By contrast, for the majorities of both rural and urban resettlers at Itaparica, and for the farmers at Nangbeto and each of the two Indian sites, economic benefits have been modest at best and minimal for most. Satisfaction ratings are correspondingly poor. These complaints override the generally positive reactions to the supply of social infrastructure. The resettlers seem to be saying that household income levels mean more to them than services and amenities. This is particularly striking in the *agrovilas* still waiting for irrigation water at Itaparica, where much-improved facilities and substantial monthly income subsidies have not offset the families' distress over having nothing to do.

Economic benefits and employment also correlate better than compensation rates with satisfaction levels. Two of the case studies show unusual associations between resettler satisfaction and the adequacy of compensation payments. At Pak Mun, the project authority compensated resettlers for affected houses and land at exceedingly generous rates, but a disproportionately high percentage (almost 60 percent) of families claim to be unsatisfied—even though on average they have not suffered any decline in income since the dam was completed. This incongruous result has several explanations. First is a genuine concern that losses to fisheries have not yet been adequately compensated. Second is a reluctance to admit improvements until the compensation controversies have been pushed as far as they can go. Third are the much less attractive resettlement options offered at the beginning of the project. Fourth are the many years of high-profile NGO protests. The last two factors have left a bitter taste despite favorable economic outcomes.

The other counterintuitive response comes from Kedung Ombo. Although controversy over compensation payments reached epic proportions, most resettlers now seem to have put that episode behind them and want to get on with advancing their already-improving household economies. This outcome is the exact opposite of Pak Mun, even though both areas are benefiting from dynamic regional growth that owes nothing to developments at the reservoir. The difference may be that at Pak Mun the resettlers were asked if they were satisfied, and at Kedung Ombo if they were satisfactorily stabilized. The latter formulation may be better for getting a more realistic appraisal.

Any question comparing satisfaction before and after the dam is bound to call forth good memories about the former lifestyle, when there was little sense of land pressure or scarcity, or long hours of work under difficult conditions. Farmers could practically throw their seed at the earth and be assured of a reasonable harvest. Fruit, vegetables, and other foods were readily available along the fertile valleys. The rivers were also filled with fish that were relatively easy to catch. With resettlement, all these people have been forced into more difficult agronomic conditions that require much better farming skills and a more intense daily work routine to prosper. They now also face the possibility that the rainfed crops will fail or their prices will fall. These differences weigh heavily on their minds when they are asked if they feel happier now.

Country Commitment and Performance Are Varied but Improving

Country performance varies, ranging from ahead of the Bank to deficient. As a group, the projects suggest an improving trend, which is confirmed by looking at subsequent projects in the study countries and efforts to put lessons to work. Greater expectations and pressure from the World Bank may explain part of the improved performance, even where government was already on a successful course.

Shuikou, Yantan, and Pak Mun exceeded World Bank standards. Although all three projects undoubtedly benefited from Bank assistance and are better than most non–Bank projects in China and Thailand, much of the credit has to go to their governments. Shuikou and Yantan set new standards in preparing for income restoration; Pak Mun set new standards in minimizing impacts through redesign and in maximizing compensation rates. These projects show what committed countries can do, and dispel any argument that resettlement cannot meet World Bank guidelines.

Itaparica—although a depressing story and headed toward an uncertain outcome—also shows how far a borrower is willing to go to meet World Bank standards. Compensation and relocation were handled efficiently. After ten years, the government still aims to complete the irrigation schemes. It would bankrupt most borrowers to do so in such an expensive way, but the striking commitment to complete at any cost—even if strongly encouraged by the Bank and Pólo—must be recognized. Nevertheless, delays in construction, primitive marketing arrangements, and a lack of vision for handling the nonviable subschemes indicate that commitment was not translated into sound design and implementation. Another project with a dam and irrigation scheme recently negotiated by the Bank and the Bahia state government—one of the two states involved at Itaparica—has a more flexible and feasible resettlement component, designed intentionally to avoid the mistakes of Itaparica.

At Kedung Ombo, country performance during the project was generally unsatisfactory. The few positive steps—such as the establishment of three new villages near the reservoir but outside the original design, and the waiver on clearing families out of the greenbelt—were more than offset by the failure to manage the compensation program to anybody's satisfaction. Inattention and indifference to resettlers' concerns led to serious conflict—and an atmosphere of coercion and intimidation. Some transmigrant communities have been waiting 12 years for promised benefits. Even so, the lessons of Kedung Ombo have guided subsequent resettlement operations by the irrigation authority, and the packages offered displaced families in new projects are now fairer and more flexible. The authority claims to have fully caught up with Bank standards.

Nangbeto is difficult case to judge. The power company did a fine job of relocation and fully expected successful resettlement. Although there were some warning signs of future population pressure, these were far enough away not to figure in resettlement planning. Lack of follow-up and little if any attention to income restoration mars performance that is satisfactory in many other regards. However, because of that lapse in attention to the overriding income objective, the resettlement component was unsatisfactory.

The two projects in India, even more troubling, represent a special category of failure. Resettlers from the Narayanpur reservoir in Karnataka are finally getting some retrofit rehabilitation, but the damage has been done and a generation of displaced persons has paid the price. Progress has been made in the past four years, especially in preparing for the early rounds of resettlement from the Almatti reservoir. In fact the project authority's recently installed computerized cadaster and evaluation program is an impressive mechanism for defining individual compensation packages. However, the previous years of neglect caused irreparable harm. People at Narayanpur cultivate significantly reduced land holdings of poorer quality—with lower yields, production, and incomes as a result. Although some have found other sources of employment, and irrigation might yet improve their lives, they should not have been put in such desperate positions. The government of Karnataka's continued routine reliance on emergency transport and metal transit sheds to relocate people is unacceptable. And the government's raising the Almatti dam again, forcing the sudden evacuation of 8,000 more people, is deplorable.

Country performance on each of the three main activities of resettlement shows the following: on compensation, ratings vary but are generally good, and poor performers appear to be improving. On relocation, the overall record is better, except for the emergency atmosphere engendered by Karnataka State's hurry-up water storage construction program. On income restoration, the performance ratings collapse. Only China warrants high marks, and even this applause must be restrained. In its comments on the draft study, the government asked the Bank to recognize the operation in Shuikou as exceptional—and not to imply that such high standards prevail throughout the country as to leave little room for improvement.

Resettler Participation Is Common at All Stages of Projects

With one striking exception, beneficiary participation in some aspects of project design and a broader set of implementation decisions was common. No households targeted for resettlement were invited to participate in the decision to build the dam, although at Pak Mun the project authority made a substantial concession to minimize protests by moving the dam upstream and lowering its height (sacrificing 33 percent of its power, but also reducing the reservoir size by 60 percent and the number of flooded people by more than 90 percent). At the two projects in China, and at Maharashtra and Nangbeto, affected farmers were brought into discussions of compensation rates, relocation, and employment options from the beginning.

In the other three projects, the authorities began with a heavy hand and relative insensitivity toward resettler preferences, but all have become conscious of the issue, moved toward participatory action, and have benefited from doing so. This was the case in Itaparica, where the farmers union, Pólo Sindical, was established even before the Bank became involved to force the power authority to accommodate resettler interests. Although relations were often strained, both sides agree that the results were positive and Pólo's contribution to developments at the site was significant. Participatory relations at Karnataka Krishna started slowly, with minimal involvement of displacees from the Narayanpur reservoir but with increasingly positive contacts at Almatti. At Pak Mun, after an initial difficult and confrontational period of two years, the authority started in 1992 to respond to resettler demands to modify the resettlement options. The increases in compensation packages that followed, raising average levels by a factor of five, were all negotiated with affected families.

The exception is Kedung Ombo, at least in the district of Kemusu, where the fight over compensation rates was concentrated. There, interaction between government and resettlers remained tense through and beyond the project period. Whether better participation was even feasible in that situation is questionable, given the historical and political bases for the confrontation.

The polar examples of participatory action—total immersion at Shuikou and exclusion at Kedung Ombo—match the outcomes of the two projects, with Shuikou the best performer in the sample and Kedung Ombo one of the worst. However, the rest of the set does not show a comfortable relationship between participation and outcome. Participatory involvement can be rated high at Itaparica and uneven but generally good at Nangbeto, while outcomes are rated low. The results are in line with expectations, however: participation contributes to good outcomes but cannot guarantee them. Since participation correlates only modestly with results, attention turns to the means of involving beneficiaries and securing adequate representation through elected and proxy leaders. The lack of effective mediation to relieve disputes appears to be a major gap in many instances.

At Itaparica, however, participatory activity became dysfunctional. Pólo's invasive presence in the unfolding drama around that lake contributed to the poor outcome of the irrigation schemes. Pólo demanded land-for-land, and the replacement land to be near the reservoir, from the beginning of its challenge to the project authority, the government, and the Bank. That was its primary platform and battle cry (*terra por terra no margem do lago*), and both demands can in hindsight be described as unsound. The shift to high-tech irrigation systems on soils that Pólo knew were risky was not a sensible solution for a large number (and perhaps for a majority) of Pólo's constituents. Flexibility on this point, and a willingness to explore other solutions with the project authority, would have been preferable. Pólo shares responsibility for having pushed doctrine beyond long-term interests.

Nongovernmental Organization Participation Is Far from Optimal

The group of projects surveyed was far from optimal in its use of NGOs. The two cases where NGO involvement was most intense were characterized by adversarial relationships and NGO advocacy but with minimum technical support. Pak Mun and Kedung Ombo were damaged by virulent relationships with NGOs that polarized borrower-resettler relationships. These acrimonious relationships have endured. While early and loud NGO criticism of plans and actions in these two resettlement operations had a profoundly positive impact on government behavior, only the Kedung Ombo project benefited from on-the-ground contributions. That NGO involvement (by an operational NGO, not the advocacy NGOs) was too brief and limited to have a substantial effect. NGO behavior at Pak Mun is most unreasonable: NGOs continue to criticize the project authority despite its efforts to accommodate resettler interests. The fishery issue is still unresolved, but that does not warrant the abuse. NGO behavior at Kedung Ombo is easier to justify, since the government took few accommodating steps.

India is the clearest case of missed opportunities. In Karnataka, an NGO based in Bangalore developed several good resettlement plans, but the state government used them only to a very limited extent. Given the NGO's reputation for effective grassroots work, this was unfortunate. Other NGOs were to assist in monitoring and evaluation, but that input has also been very limited. In Maharashtra, the state government used NGOs to develop rehabilitation plans for the retrofit operation, but the key income-generating scheme component has not yet begun. Both state governments could have used NGOs much more effectively, especially in soliciting resettler participation and in designing and implementing the income-generation components.

Some observers refer to Pólo Sindical as an NGO, and take credit on behalf of NGOs for Pólo's involvement at Itaparica. Moving Pólo from the list of NGOs to the list of participants removes the only example of significant grass roots involvement in the study.

Good Relations between Resettlers and Host Communities

Relations between resettlers and host communities were surprisingly good in all but one project. Given the additional pressures and scarcities that an influx of resettlers produces, host communities generally responded with sympathy and understanding. Geography helps explain this benign outcome, because the inundated villages lay in a string pattern along the rivers, usually with few other villages above them. That association breaks down, of course, when resettlers are transported long distances to other fertile areas, but this happened only with the transmigrants from Kedung Ombo. A conflict with hosts appeared in one of the transmigration sites. The only significant resettler-host conflict close to the reservoirs was at Nangbeto, and that was only after years had passed. And the Nangbeto conflict can be partly attributed to inadequate efforts by the power company to facilitate a smooth transition. The authority and the government failed to provide incentives to the host communities. Even so, the hosts accepted the resettlers and provided them with land for cultivation until they themselves began to run short of land and suffer during the economic crisis.

There are no signs that hosts considered themselves left behind by the advantages provided to resettlers. At Pak Mun, unaffected people have clamored for inclusion in the generous compensation packages on the flimsiest of excuses, but these are neighbors and lifelong friends of the affected people and not hosts to inbound migrants.

Costs Vary Among Projects

Average costs expended by the project per resettled family range from $6,000[3] at Nangbeto to $185,000 at Itaparica. Nangbeto has the lowest costs precisely because nothing was done to help establish alternative production systems and there were no land compensation costs. Itaparica stands out because it includes large expenses unique to the sample, such as nine years of income supplements, the costs of periodic demobilization and remobilization of crews and equipment, adjustments to contracts to match raging inflation, and the extraordinarily expensive irrigation system. These are entirely provisional figures, certain to understate total costs because expenditures by nonproject agencies—from the provincial agricultural services' regular budgets, for example—are excluded, as are out-of-pocket costs to the resettlers. The figures have an apples and oranges quality, because of the very different profiles of expenditure categories. Even so, the orders of magnitude of all but the Itaparica scheme are within the range usually projected, with Kedung Ombo at $7,000 and Pak Mun at $11,600. Shuikou's $24,000 is higher because most of the towns and villages had to be completely rebuilt—some on terraces carved out of hillsides. It would be higher still if all the investment costs of the town and village industries were included. This would be the appropriate course to take to classify this scheme—as it should be classified—as a regional development program.

The Main Lessons Learned Focus on the Difference between Results and Plans, the Limited Capacity of Public Agencies, Resettlement Compensation, and Borrower Commitment

Results, Not Plans, Are the Appropriate Touchstone for Quality Management

In the cases examined, planning received disproportionate attention in comparison with results. This is the downside of the otherwise positive progress with planning. While better planning usually translates into better implementation, this assumption has not held up for involuntary resettlement. As a subsidiary operation, resettlement continues to receive inadequate attention during implementation.

Public Agencies, for the Most Part, Are Limited in their Capacity to Handle Resettlement

In most of the cases, public sector agencies mishandled or ignored resettlement. However, the two projects in China show how resettlement can work when executing agencies are prepared to use any tools and take whatever opportunities are available. What China does can be done by others. The Pak Mun and Kedung Ombo cases, where resettlers were picked up and carried along by tidal changes in the regional economy even without planning, confirm that planners can be more aggressive in designing compensation packages linked to non-land-based diversification strategies to put displacees back to work.

Offering Resettlers Land-for-Land Is an Option for Income Restoration, but Not the Only One

Pursuing land-for-land policies where the circumstances are unfavorable will produce unsatisfactory results, as they did at Itaparica. Governments have had difficulty finding ways to compensate for losses of cultivable land by providing comparable farm holdings nearby. The alternatives have been equally disappointing. Governments had difficulty establishing, with or without donor support, other bases for productive employment. In retrospect, the two tasks are among the most challenging in development: big dam sites usually eliminate the most productive farming systems in the neighborhood, while the people in the flooded valleys have few skills and less motivation to shift to other activities. While land-for-land should be given due consideration and appropriate analysis, it should not be adopted regardless of costs.

Genuine Borrower Commitment to Doing Resettlement Well Is the Key to Success.

Bland assurances, conveniently forgotten, guarantee failure. However, differentiating between genuine and false commitment is never an easy job. Equally, the capacity to deliver should be appraised realistically, and arrangements for independent monitoring and evaluation should be built in from the outset. Fortunately, governments are becoming more committed to good resettlement performance. In two cases among the six countries in the study, borrowers exceed Bank standards and are leading and teaching the Bank.

There are many levels of commitment. Sometimes there is commitment at higher, more policy-oriented levels but relatively less at the resettlement officer level, where the resettlement posting is sometimes viewed as an undesirable two-year career step. At other times dedicated individuals in the field are frustrated by indifference at higher levels, which robs them of the resources and other needs to perform effectively. Another problem was highlighted at Kedung Ombo, where the provincial and regency governments never accepted full ownership of the resettlement program after the central government authorities disengaged. At Nangbeto, too, responsibilities could not be successfully transferred as planned to local government services.

In all circumstances, adequate resource allocations are essential, and they must outlast the construction period. The government's commitments on the budget side have to be maintained, and this is precisely where countries must come up with imaginative ideas if resettlement is to work.

Notes

1. Environmental Department, *Regional Remedial Action Planning for Involuntary Resettlement in World Bank Supported Projects: A Report on One Year of Follow-up to Resettlement and Development*, Washington, D.C., World Bank, Environmental Department, 1995, p. 6.
2. Operations Evaluation Department, 1993, *Early Experience with Involuntary Resettlement: Overview*, Report No. 12142, World Bank, Operations Evaluation Department (OED). Annex A contained a table based on a brief review of evaluation reports of recently completed projects involving resettlement operations. Of the 47 projects for which a determination could be made, including the four case study projects in the Operations Evaluation Department sample, 27 were found satisfactory and 20 were found unsatisfactory, p. iv.
3. All dollar amounts are U.S. dollars.

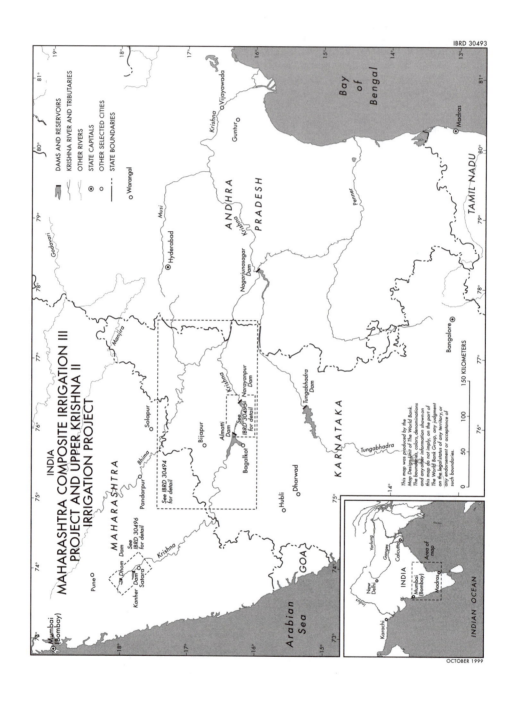

IBRD 30493

INDIA

MAHARASHTRA COMPOSITE IRRIGATION III
PROJECT AND UPPER KRISHNA II
IRRIGATION PROJECT

DAMS AND RESERVOIRS
KRISHNA RIVER AND TRIBUTARIES
OTHER RIVERS
⊙ STATE CAPITALS
○ OTHER SELECTED CITIES
STATE BOUNDARIES

Arabian Sea

MAHARASHTRA

Mumbai (Bombay)

Pune ○

Dhom Dam
See IBRD 30496
for detail
Kanher Dam
Satara

Krishna

Bhima

Pandarpur ○

Solapur ○

Bijapur ○

Dharwad ○

Hubli ○

Almatti Dam

Bagalkot ○

See IBRD 30495
for detail

Narayanpur Dam

See IBRD 30494
for detail

KARNATAKA

Tungabhadra

Tungabhadra Dam

GOA

Bangalore ⊙

Manjira

Godavari

Hyderabad ⊙

Musi

ANDHRA PRADESH

Krishna

Nagarjunasagar Dam

Krishna

Guntur ○

Vijayawada ○

○ Warangal

Penner

Bay
of
Bengal

TAMIL NADU

Madras ⊙

0   50   100   150 KILOMETERS

This map was produced by the
Map Design Unit of The World Bank.
The boundaries, colors, denominations
and any other information shown on
this map do not imply, on the part of
The World Bank Group, any judgment
on the legal status of any territory, or
any endorsement or acceptance of
such boundaries.

INDIA

New Delhi ○

Indus

Karachi ○

Ganges

Yarlung

Calcutta ○

Mumbai (Bombay) ○

Madras ○

Area of
map

INDIAN OCEAN

OCTOBER 1999

2

Confrontations and Crises
in Upper Krishna

The driving force behind the Upper Krishna project of the state government of Karnataka, India, is the year 2000 deadline for determining watersharing of the Krishna river among the three states through which it flows. The Interstate Water Tribunal will agree on each state's share of water rights on the basis of water use, as demonstrated by completion of water storage facilities (the reservoirs). Since use of the Krishna's water is of tremendous importance to all three drought-prone states, all desire to maximize their claims.

Given the primacy of moving ahead with completion and filling of the reservoirs, the Government of Karnataka relegated resettlement to a low priority and proved unwilling to shift resources from dam construction to relocation and rehabilitation when progress on the latter fell behind. The World Bank placed pressure on the state government to focus on resettlement in every way the Bank could. It delayed its Upper Krishna II project three years, until the government showed progress on the legal framework, institutional capacity, and income restoration. When project compliance faltered, the Bank twice suspended the project and insisted on remedial actions before lifting suspension. However, despite the Bank's intense efforts and scrutiny, the state government dragged its heels in making corrections. Clearly, even the Bank's firmest resettlement principles are no substitute for strong government commitment.

Nor did the state government heed the complaints of resettlers, although the vast majority of them went to court over inadequate compensation, and won. Only in 1995, when dam construction was nearly finished and reservoirs were filling, did it make a serious effort to correct the deficiencies in compensation and income restoration. However, even after that, it allowed resevoir level increases that caused flooding of villages and forced emergency relocation of thousands of villagers—not once, but twice.

TABLE 2.1
Project Chronology

Date	Event
1962	Upper Krishna Project begins.
1972	Preliminary notification for house and land acquisition begins at Narayanpur with compensation approved.
1978	World Bank Karnataka Irrigation Project is approved.
1978	Resettlement begins at Narayanpur.
1979	Resettlement proceeds slowly: only 7% of land is acquired, and 12% of new village construction is completed.
1982	Narayanpur reservoir filling begins. Some coercion is used to move villagers.
1983–84	Compensation payments are completed for people affected by Narayanpur.
1986	Only 18,000 people have been resettled, leaving 21,000 to be moved.
1986	Karnataka Irrigation Project ends.
1989	Upper Krishna II project is approved.
1992	World Bank suspends disbursements because of an inadequate rehabilitation program.
1993	Government of Karnataka implements supplementary ex gratia (supplemental compensation) payments to resettlers.
1994, Feb.	Government of Karnataka meets Bank conditions for project continuation.
1994	Relocation begins at Almatti.
1995, Sept.	World Bank suspends project again, except for resettlement component, because of low disbursements for resettlement and relocation.
1995, Oct.	A new Secretary of Rehabilitation and Land Acquisition is named and many improvements instituted to accelerate relocation and rehabilitation progress, but disbursements still lag.
1996, Jan.	A consent award system is adopted, which provides extra compensation to resettlers who agree not to go to court over compensation payment.
1996, summer	Narayanpur reservoir is filled and all settlers are relocated; 20,000 people at Almatti are flooded out of their homes and relocated to transit sheds while resettlement shelters are under construction.
1996, Nov.	World Bank and the Government of Karnataka agree to lift the project suspension and extend closing date by 6 months.
1996–97	Houseplot distribution and home construction proceed quickly.
1997	Government of Karnataka raises the spillway at Almatti Dam in violation of the agreement with the World Bank, resulting in emergency relocation of 8,000 people flooded out during the summer monsoon.
1997, June	Upper Krishna II project closes.

Government Commitment Is Critical

The Krishna River is one of three main rivers on the Indian subcontinent, originating in the state of Maharashtra and flowing east through Karnataka and Andhra Pradesh before emptying into the Bay of Bengal (map IBRD 30493). The Upper Krishna Project, which will eventually irrigate more than half a million hectares, is vital to the future of agriculture in the drought-prone regions of

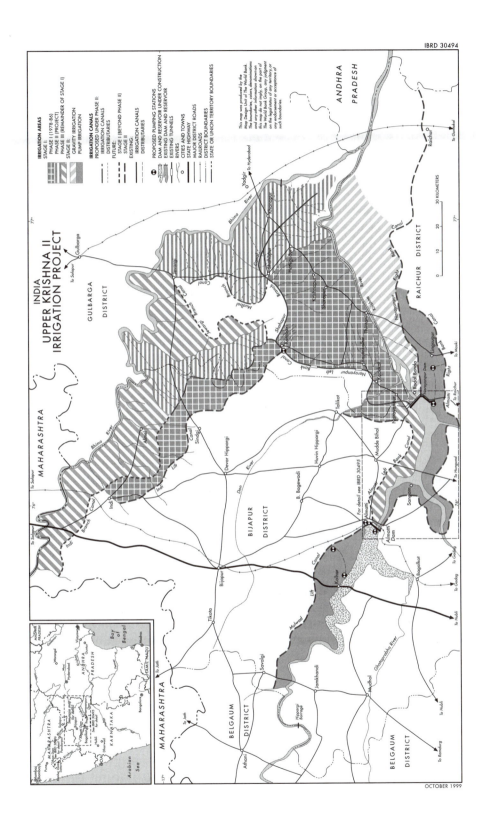

IBRD 30494

INDIA
UPPER KRISHNA II
IRRIGATION PROJECT

IRRIGATION AREAS
STAGE I:
PHASE I (1978-86)
PHASE II (PROJECT)
PHASE III (REMAINDER OF STAGE I)
STAGE II:
GRAVITY IRRIGATION
PUMP IRRIGATION

IRRIGATION CANALS
PROPOSED UNDER PHASE II:
IRRIGATION CANALS
DISTRIBUTARIES
FUTURE:
STAGE I (BEYOND PHASE II)
STAGE II
EXISTING:
IRRIGATION CANALS
DISTRIBUTARIES

PROPOSED PUMPING STATIONS
DAM AND RESERVOIR UNDER CONSTRUCTION
EXISTING DAM AND RESERVOIR
EXISTING TUNNELS
RIVERS
CITIES AND TOWNS
STATE HIGHWAY
MAJOR DISTRICT ROADS
RAILROADS
DISTRICT BOUNDARIES
STATE OR UNION TERRITORY BOUNDARIES

This map was produced by the
Map Design Unit of The World Bank.
The boundaries, colors, denominations
and any other information shown on
this map do not imply, on the part of
The World Bank Group, any judgment
on the legal status of any territory, or
any endorsement or acceptance of
such boundaries.

OCTOBER 1999

northern Karnataka. The multi-phase, multi-stage project requires the construction of two dams: Narayanpur and, immediately upstream of the Narayanpur reservoir, Almatti (map IBRD 30494). The Upper Krishna Project started in 1962 and is still not close to completion (table 2.1).

The World Bank assisted the state government's project with the Karnataka Irrigation Project, 1978 to 1986; and the Upper Krishna Irrigation Project, 1989 to 1997. Narayanpur Reservoir was completely filled by 1996, and all resettlers were relocated. The Almatti Dam was not to be completed until 1998 at the earliest. Relocation at Almatti started in 1994, but most resettlers can still cultivate their former lands, so they have not yet experienced the full effect of resettlement.

The state's project lacked preconditions for successful resettlement. Political will, a legal framework, institutional capacity, adequate budget, comprehensive planning, a development program, and participation of the affected population were all absent. Violations of government commitments resulted in successive project suspensions. Finally, in 1995, resettlement performance began to turn around. Land compensation rates now approach market prices. Supplemental payments help make up for past deficiencies. Resettlement is now more participatory. However, a generation of resettlers on the Upper Krishna paid a high price.

Dams Flood 880 Square Kilometers, with 240,000 People Affected

Narayanpur is a composite dam ten kilometers long, with a 1,023 meter central cement section, and 31 meters high. It lies in a flat, broad valley; consequently small changes in elevation flood large parcels of land. The reservoir is 50 kilometers long and covers approximately 132 square kilometers. Almatti Dam is also a composite dam, 1,159 meters long, and 39 meters high. The reservoir, when filled, will have a surface area of 750 square kilometers.

The Upper Krishna Project contains many resettlement components. The number of resettlers involved will not be known until the Almatti reservoir, canals, and roads are completed. According to the most recent estimates, Narayanpur affected 90 villages, required the resettlement of approximately 5,100 households, and submerged at least part of the lands of another 1,433 households (map IBRD 30495) for a total of 36,306 people. The Bank part of the Almatti project will affect 95 villages, 32,673 households, and 142,525 people. Another 2,602 households (16,000 people) have been or will be affected by the 96 square kilometers of canals, drains, and roads. Accounting for underestimates, the total number of affected people may be 240,000.

The Government of Karnataka has even bigger plans. The Inter-State Water Tribunal, which allocates water from the Krishna River among the three riparian states—Maharashtra, Karnataka, and Andhra Pradesh—is set to meet again in the year 2000. Karnataka's share of the water will be determined by the percentage of water it is using at that time, as measured by the amount of water stored in reservoirs. Committed to obtaining as large a share of the Krishna's water as

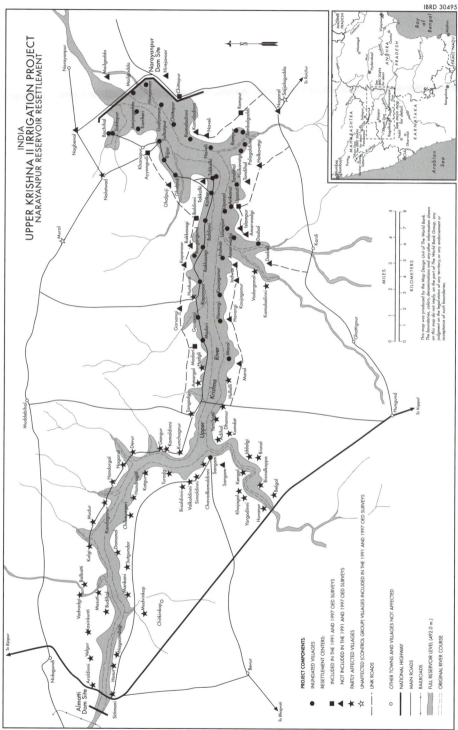

IBRD 30495

OCTOBER 1999

possible, the state government has built and plans to install radial gates above the present spillway to further elevate the Almatti reservoir. That would increase the reservoir volume sixfold, more than triple the submerged area, and add 150,000 to 200,000 people to the number of those affected by the Bank assisted part of the project.

Implementation of Resettlement—an Abysmal Record

Physical relocation of the families affected by Narayanpur did not go according to plan. Resettlement began in 1978 but proceeded slowly as dam construction and reservoir filling lagged. By June 1979 only seven percent of the land had been acquired, 12 percent of the compensation for buildings had been paid, and 12 percent of the new resettlement villages had been completed. Many families did not move until the last possible moment after the reservoir began filling in 1982. Filling of the reservoir was not completed for another 14 years, although 100 square kilometers of the reservoir were filled within four years. By 1986, only 2,925 families (18,000 people) had been resettled. This left a backlog of 3,500 families (21,000 people) at Narayanpur.

Since the new villages offered practically no means of livelihood, people preferred to use their existing facilities for as long as possible. While the physical infrastructure of new villages was an improvement over the old villages, replacement of lost agricultural land and other productive assets was left up to the resettlers. Because compensation was inadequate, 80 to 90 percent of the people losing land could not buy any replacement land, and those that did generally owned less land, and land of poorer quality. Since the reservoir was only partly filled, and some of that for only part of the year, many people continued to farm the drawdown area. Most new villages are only one to two kilometers from the old villages, so distances to farms did not significantly increase. About 40 percent of the submerged lands could still be farmed year round, and another 30 percent were uncovered for at least three to four months each year, when one crop could be harvested. Most of the remaining resettlers sought work as agricultural laborers or migrated.

Only with the design of the second-phase project were the resettlement failures fully recognized. The Karnataka Irrigation Project had no resettlement plan, no estimate of the number of people that would ultimately be affected, a grossly inadequate budget, no institutional capacity to move anything close to the necessary number of people, no income restoration strategy, completely inadequate legal frameworks, and very limited political will to improve resettlement and rehabilitation. The results were predictable. Most people affected by Narayanpur suffered a deterioration in their standard of living; landless laborers have been particularly hard hit. Meanwhile, at Almatti, about 13,000 households had been at least partly compensated, but only 354 had moved (submergence had not yet started). The rest had largely consumed their compensation, and would be in a predicament once they had to move.

It took three years after the Karnataka Irrigation Project ended to meet preconditions for the second project, Upper Krishna II, to be approved. The Bank insisted on a pilot project for 500 households. The resettlement budget was tripled, to $60 million. However, the project ran into difficulties immediately. Of 2,315 households to be rehabilitated at Narayanpur in fiscal 1991, only 40 had been rehabilitated by October 1990, a two percent achievement rate. To be fair, only two percent of physical works were achieved, but resettlement was supposed to catch up with civil works construction.

After marginal improvements in early 1991, resettlement performance deteriorated quickly. By July, only 397 households were rehabilitated, leaving a backlog of 2,266. Continued Bank support of the project was predicated on remedial actions. As far as resettlement and rehabilitation were concerned, the Government of Karnataka had not taken any positive steps to comply with Bank recommendations. On November 3, 1992, the Bank suspended disbursements.

The Bank set benchmarks as conditions for lifting the suspension and resuming disbursements. These included new mechanisms for ensuring equitable compensation and several new supplemental payments to redress past inadequacies of compensation. Progress was sufficient to justify the Bank's partly lifting the suspension on February 16, 1993. It took until February 1994 for the Bank to fully lift the suspension.

Progress started to deteriorate again in 1995, and the project was suspended—except for disbursements for resettlement expenses—for the second time. Despite unparalleled attention to resettlement and rehabilitation, disbursements totaled only $1.4 million during the next year. As the project neared its completion date of December 31, 1996, efforts were intensified to meet the conditions to lift the suspension and thus extend the closing date.

Given the intense efforts to catch up with dam construction, resettlement implementation accelerated significantly in the last year. In the five months from October 1996 to March 1997, house plot distribution increased 60 percent, houses under construction increased 82 percent, and houses completed increased 113 percent, over totals as of October 1996. Disbursement of compensation and other grants also increased.

The state government then violated the main condition of the agreement. It raised the spillway three meters to maintain its schedule of raising the dam to 524 meters above sea level by 1998. This required the relocation of 8,000 more people under emergency conditions during the 1997 summer monsoon floods—fewer than in 1996, when 20,000 people were flooded out of their homes. People were rescued from their houses by boats and helicopters as a one-in-ten-year flood swept through the valley. The evacuees were placed in temporary metal transit sheds while they continued construction on their permanent houses in the resettlement centers. Life is very difficult in the metal sheds, as people's health suffers, much of the village infrastructure is not complete, and the population is inadequate to support shops, services, and other amenities. A year later many were still living in the metal sheds because they lacked the financial means to complete their permanent houses to a sufficient stage to inhabit them. In response to that latest violation, the Bank closed the project on June 30, 1997.

Compensation—Too Little, Too Late, and Too Contentious

The original framework for land acquisition and resettlement in India is the Land Acquisition Act of 1894. Compensation consists of three parts.

- Compensation for the market value of assets acquired (land and structures).
- A solatium (a premium paid because of the compulsory nature of the acquisition).
- Interest on the compensation if it is not paid at the time of acquisition.

The basic principle is to pay the market value of assets acquired on the date of preliminary notification. An additional 15 percent of the determined market value was paid as solatium. Interest for delayed payment of compensation was set at five percent per year.

Government Continually Modifies Compensation Policy

Because of increasing land prices, lengthy delays during an inflationary period, and other problems, the policy has been modified almost every year since the mid-1980s, as described below.

Increased Land Compensation

This was the single largest change due to increasing land prices. In 1978, land compensation was $380 per acre at prevailing exchange rates. By 1985, the rate was $1,021. By 1986, it was $1,368.

Increased Solatium and Interest on Delayed Compensation Payments

In 1984, the solatium was doubled to 30 percent. The interest rate was increased from five percent to nine percent for the first year and to 15 percent for subsequent years.

Consent Awards

To reduce the number of cases going to court, the Government of Karnataka adopted a compensation system based on consent awards, whereby the compensation payment for land is enhanced in exchange for resettler agreement not to dispute the award in court. Consent awards in 1997 ranged from $1,408 to $1,521 per acre for dryland, and $2,143 to $2,429 for irrigated land. The resettlers not only benefit from better compensation rates, they also avoid the effort and expenses of hiring lawyers or others to pursue their cases in court, which absorbs up to 40 percent of the court-ordered enhancement. Therefore, land compensation rates have increased significantly (in local currency). This does not necessarily equal replacement costs, however, as land prices could escalate faster than compensation rates.

Ex Gratia Payments

Several forms of ex gratia payments as compensation for housing, land, and income generation have begun in the past few years to help rehabilitate resettlers. The house construction grants are $629 per household. Land purchase grants range from $571 to $1,714, depending on the amount of land lost and land remaining. The income-generating scheme grants range up to $571. Everyone eligible for these ex gratia payments should receive them, no matter when they originally were compensated or moved. Those losing more than ten hectares received nothing beyond cash compensation for lost assets. (These resettlers were considered sufficiently well off not to require rehabilitation assistance).

Resettlement Packages to Adult Dependents

This change granted houseplot, housing compensation, and ex gratia payments to sons aged 18 or older and unmarried daughters aged 35 or older and still living with their parents. A major problem is that the sizes of all these grants are fixed and not indexed to inflation, so their value has significantly eroded over time.

Compensation Is Inadequate

Preliminary notification for land and house acquisition at Narayanpur began in 1971, with compensation first issued in 1972. Compensation payments were completed, except for a few special cases, by fiscal 1984. Resettlement has been a very extended process, with people not moving until rising waters in the reservoir forced them to leave their houses. For example, among 220 households surveyed in 1997, notification occurred between 1972 and 1987, and people relocated between 1979 and 1993. Thus, different people were subject to very different compensation policies.

Compensation rates for Narayanpur resettlers were not generous, and the long gap between receipt of compensation and actual abandonment of the property meant that compensation money had already been spent and none remained to buy replacement land and houses. Compensation payments were often received in installments, so resettlers had difficulty accumulating enough cash at any one time to buy replacement houses or land. Those that received adequate compensation and bought replacement land immediately appear to be doing well.

While most resettlers eventually found the means to replace their houses, they have not been able to buy adequate replacement land. Finally, except for the grants designed to generate income, which so far have been too little and too late to make much of a difference, nothing has been done to compensate for lost incomes. For example, the landless are not entitled to any land compensation, yet their incomes are often affected because there is much less opportunity for agricultural labor work among villages that lost most of their land.

The Uses of Compensation Vary

Use of compensation money varied by village. In fact, a residual category—other expenditures—accounted for 36 percent of all compensation in six surveyed villages. The next largest use, 26 percent, was for buying land, although this varied by village from 10 to 34 percent. The next largest use, 20 percent, was for social activities. Compensation gave resettlers an opportunity to amass a sizable amount of money at one time for weddings and dowries. Loan repayment was also a significant (14 percent) use of compensation money. Often, however, resettlers accumulated increased debt because of impoverishment caused by resettlement.

The use of the ex gratia payments has been significantly different from use of the original compensation because these funds are allocated for specific purposes. For the land purchase grants, 67 of the 74 sample households that were eligible purchased land. Unfortunately, most of the land bought is far from the villages and has to be leased out. Practically all households were using the housing ex gratia payments to expand or improve their houses. Only the income-generating grants are not being used much, partly because their small size ($571 or less) makes them unattractive options. So far they are mainly used to buy milk animals, sheep, bullocks and bullock carts, and a few enterprises (for example, flour milling), but the numbers are small.

Income Restoration Depends Too Much on Irrigation

The major income restoration strategy was to move people into the irrigation command (map IBRD 30494). As land became irrigated, farmers were expected to sell off extra land as the irrigated land absorbed their available labor. Another strategy was to provide resettlers with government jobs. Many income-generating schemes were envisioned, including dairy cattle, bullocks and bullock carts, sheep rearing, sericulture, fishing, poultry, and small enterprises.

Unfortunately, the income-generating strategies were not implemented, and the expected quantities of land in the command area did not materialize. The principal strategy of moving people into the command area has not been implemented, mainly because the command areas are still in the early stages of development, long after resettlers were displaced. The command areas themselves are sources of outmigration because of land pressure. Only when it became abundantly clear by the early 1990s that this was completely inadequate were more deliberate measures taken to do something about income restoration.

Some resettler villages have been able to develop irrigation schemes. When

TABLE 2.2
Annual Household Incomes

Sources of income (dollars per household in the previous 12 months)[a]	Affected villages			Unaffected villages	
	1991	1993	1997	1991	1997
Number of households surveyed	210	210	224	60	60
Farm-income		228	318		408
Nonfarm income		290	198		375
Total income	640	518	516	944	783

[a] All income figures are converted at the 1997 exchange rate of 35 rupees = one dollar and are adjusted for 23 percent inflation from 1991–93 and 30 percent inflation from 1993–97.

they are completed, large-scale canal irrigation schemes under construction on both banks of the Narayanpur Reservoir could significantly boost incomes. The state government established a large fish nursery, but the reservoir fishery has not been well developed because of the lack of an ice factory and marketing, among other reasons. The income generating scheme grants led to some additional income, but very little diversification. Income restoration is by far the weakest aspect of resettlement.

Income Impact Trends Are Similar to Those in Unaffected Areas

No baseline studies of the affected villages were undertaken before resettlement began. However, data collected since the first surveys indicate income trends (table 2.2).[1]

The resettlement villages have moved beyond the declining-income phase to the income-stabilization phase, largely because of villagers' own efforts. At least this is an improvement over the earlier period, 1991–93, when current incomes held steady but fell 20 percent in real terms.

Without baseline data on preresettlement incomes, the second best alternative is to compare resettler incomes with those in unaffected villages. Average household income in the two unaffected villages surveyed decreased by 20 percent in the six year period.[2] That resettler villages' income declines were no worse than these two relatively prosperous villages is encouraging, even if income levels remain one-third less.

Because the reservoir reached its peak level only in 1996, it is premature to determine what the final impact of the reservoir will be. So far, irrigation, increasing crop intensity, and higher crop prices appear largely to have offset the decrease in cropping area. Wage labor outside the villages also helped to increase incomes. The income-generating strategy envisioned during project planning is only belatedly coming to fruition (and then only partly).

Living Conditions Are Better, but Health Is a Worrisome Exception

Resettled villagers enjoy better electrification, water supply, transportation, and education services. Electrification increased from 42 percent of households in 1993 to 69 percent in 1997. Resettler villages, which before dam construction relied on the river or open wells for water supply, now have schemes based on piped-water, mini-water, or borewell supplies. The Government of Karnataka significantly upgraded village access roads and internal roads, resulting in better public transportation. The old villages had few educational facilities, but all the new villages have schools.

The health situation is a mixed bag. Water-related diseases, such as cholera and dysentery, are decreasing as a result of improved water sources. On the other hand, malaria has increased in all the surveyed resettler villages except the one farthest from the edge of the reservoir. The reported incidence of malaria at Narayanpur increased 15–fold from 1991 to 1996. It tripled at Almatti during the same period. This is in stark contrast to the unaffected villages—farther back from the lake—where malaria is decreasing and is not a significant problem.

The government provided limited services: a fishery, stocking the reservoir with fish, and visiting health professionals. The income-generating grants do not come with training, advisory services, or anything else, which might explain their relative lack of success so far. Resettlers do not receive the agricultural extension they need either for dryland farming or for managing irrigation. Many services that could make a difference are not provided.

The Move Hurts Women More Than Men

The project did not address gender concerns, but the 1997 household survey took pains to determine specific project impacts on women. Many more women thought their lives had worsened (65 percent) than improved (21 percent). More than five times as many women said they were less happy now than in the old village. This margin is even more negative when stratified by age, since younger women saw opportunities, while older women were losing earning capacity and were more emotionally attached to the old village. Most women (62 percent) thought they had less personal disposable income than in the old village. This has significance beyond the income loss alone, as the decisionmaking power of a woman is closely related to her personal disposable income. Labor opportunities for women were reduced. Their income from farming and livestock decreased and they became more dependent on wage income. The availability of fuelwood and fodder decreased. Livestock had to be sold. Women had to migrate for work.

Resettler Attitudes Show Memory of Years of Hardship Are Not Erased by Recent Improvements

Resettlers have always agreed about their dissatisfaction with compensation rates. A 1986 Food and Agriculture Organization report observed that 90 percent of resettlers contested compensation rates. In 1991 more than 95 percent of the households said they were dissatisfied with the initial compensation amounts for land and houses. Recent improvements in compensation such as the ex gratia payments are welcome, but do not fundamentally redress past grievances. The housing ex gratia payments are sufficient for house repair and expansion, but not for new houses. The income generating grants are too small for most productive investments. Nonetheless, the ex gratia payments and grants are sufficiently popular to encourage resettlers left with more than ten hectares (and thus ineligible) to want to be included.

The resettlers are also upset at the compensation process. They believe that it is rife with corruption, with officials, lawyers, and even NGOs taking a portion of the compensation for themselves—usually 10 to 40 percent—in exchange for assistance in processing claims.

Resettlers' lives were very difficult for the first few years after displacement and even in 1997 they saw their lives as worse in many ways: 68 percent rated themselves worse off and only 21 percent rated themselves better off. Many people who were previously self-sufficient now have to buy food. Food prices have increased. The reduction in available grazing land, previously plentiful, as well as less intercropping, meant less fodder, and led to a reduction in some livestock holdings. People had to migrate to supplement their incomes, with increasing family separation and all the other social costs of migration. Some people have not coped well with their new lives as resettlers, and drinking problems have increased.

Because additional efforts are being made to more fully rehabilitate them, resettlers tend to downplay benefits and overstate suffering in an attempt to win more benefits. Nonetheless, they generally accept that the worst is behind them. Their "resettlement centers" have stabilized as normal villages, there is better community infrastructure (clinics, centers, roads, electricity), schools are more accessible and educational quality is improving, and the resettlers' incomes and expenditures are now stabilizing or recovering (although still not what they used to be).

Federal Government Shows No Commitment

India's federal system makes resettlement a state responsibility. The federal government has no policy on involuntary resettlement, which is an obstacle to better resettlement performance. In fact, the differing resettlement laws, institutions, and capabilities of the various states is part of the problem, and Karnataka has a history as one of the worst-performing states on resettlement.

The first resettlement plan was not even prepared until July 1986—and then it was done only at Bank insistence, to facilitate approval of the follow-on project. One main problem was that until 1995, the Irrigation Department was in charge of resettlement. The needs of resettlement were usually subordinated to irrigation priorities—and still are. To ensure its rights to its share of the Krishna River, which it plans to do, the Karnataka government needs to complete the dam, fill the reservoir, and use the water by the year 2000, regardless of progress on resettlement by that time.

It is ironic that people were displaced to store water to supply the irrigation canals in the command area, but because many command areas are not yet close to completion, much of the water stored in the reservoirs is not currently used. Irrigation development is lagging reservoir filling and displacement by up to ten years, not one to two years as expected. The canals that have been built are poorly maintained—causing seepage, salinization, and additional displacement. The breakdown of the water storage-command development linkage has largely vitiated the principal income restoration strategy and contributed to unnecessary additional hardships.

In 1987, the state government began issuing orders that seemed to significantly improve the compensation package and resettlement policy. Translating these edicts into results on the ground was another matter. Resettlement still seriously lagged dam construction when the Bank first suspended disbursements in 1992. Even while the project was suspended, work continued on the dam. It was only the threat of seriously damaging relations with the Bank that led the government to make a substantial effort to improve performance in the field. In 1993, it issued the orders covering ex gratia payments and grants, improving rehabilitation significantly.

In 1995, with the appointment of a new Secretary for Rehabilitation and Land Acquisition, Upper Krishna Project, the situation began to change. Resettlement staffing increased from 150 to 900. Tens of thousands of families started construction on their homes. Thousands of ex gratia payments and grants were paid. The consent-award system was introduced. Land compensation rates finally caught up to market prices. Corrupt resettlement officers were fired. Beneficiary participation is reaching reasonable levels. Much other essential work has also been accomplished. The adoption of the consent-award system in January 1996, was a key turning point in moving beyond the previously adversarial approach. In fact, more was accomplished at Almatti between October 1995 and June 1997 than up to 1995.

Despite recent improvements, the main resettlement policy objective of income restoration was not achieved for many years, if at all (lack of baseline data prevents a firm conclusion). Planning was highly inadequate, and implementation lagged unacceptably. Recent improvements will help those not yet resettled, but offer little mitigation for those resettled under inferior arrangements. The state government fell so far behind in the first 18 years of the project that it has been forced into the untenable position of having to move people under emergency conditions as a standard operating procedure. Nothing can be done to undo the "lost generation" problem.

Ignored by the Authorities, Villagers Resorted to Courts

There was limited participation by resettlers until recently. Before 1995, the primary way for villagers to make themselves heard was to go to court contesting inadequate compensation. *By 1997, 96 percent of all resettlers had taken their cases to court.* The courts almost always awarded the resettlers additional compensation, usually about equal to the original amount, thus doubling their compensation. Even with the enhancements, resettlers were rarely able to buy land or houses of the same size and quality.

That has changed. Government of Karnataka resettlement officers now periodically conduct *gram sabhas* (village meetings) to identify affected people, select resettlement village sites and individual plots, and determine rehabilitation needs. Resettlers at Almatti report high levels of participation, including weekly meetings, consultations on most issues, and genuine responsiveness to resettlers' suggestions and preferences. This is in stark contrast to Narayanpur, where the Government of Karnataka neither expected nor provided for resettler participation. It is now too late for the Narayanpur resettlers because resettlement is essentially complete.

Nongovernment Organization Assistance Is Local and Limited

Almost all NGO activity has been by local organizations, mostly working on social welfare and income-generating activities. Only after 1996 did advocacy NGOs become involved in working for resettler's rights and fighting corruption.

Host Communities Are Sympathetic

Relations with host communities are good. The host populations are sympathetic to the plight of the resettlers. Most resettlers moved less than five kilometers. In most cases, villages were rebuilt with the same membership. It was much more typical for resettlers to move into the area of partly affected villages than of unaffected villages, so there was some shared understanding of the difficulties.

Conclusions

The resettlement operation at Upper Krishna has made one of the most dramatic turnarounds of any resettlement operation in a Bank-assisted project, from crisis and two suspensions to aproaching satisfactory performance. For the first time in a sad 20–year history, the building blocks of an acceptable resettlement program—political will, a legal framework, institutional capacity, adequate budget, comprehensive planning, a development program, and participation of the affected population—appear to be in place. The experience offers many lessons.

The planning and appraisal process was a lesson in what not to do. None of the preconditions for resettlement was in place. Not even the number of affected people was known. The Bank insisted on a pilot project, but did not wait for the results before approving the Upper Krishna project. Success in the pilot did not ensure success in the much larger-scale, full resettlement effort, which was mismanaged so badly that the project had to be suspended twice and rebuilt almost from scratch.

The entire compensation process was highly inadequate, at least until recently, and caused lasting problems. People were not compensated at replacement costs, so they were unable to replace their income-producing assets, mainly land, and had to turn to other sources of income. Delays in receiving compensation, as well as being paid in installments, further aggravated the problem. The time, effort, and money (sometimes bribes) needed to obtain compensation ate away at the already inadequate compensation.

The relocation process was poorly coordinated. Relocation was guided much more by dam-construction priorities than by rational planning. Irrigation in the command area was not coordinated with providing resettlers with irrigated lands. People have been compensated years before relocation was necessary, thus creating a complete disjuncture in the process. At other times they have had to flee rising waters during the summer monsoon.

The income restoration strategy was highly flawed. The command area was a net outmigration area, and people were not willing to sell their land on anywhere near the scale necessary to absorb resettlers. Providing income-generating grants was no substitute for thinking about how people could use that money.

Services for resettlers were highly inadequate. There were far too few health-care personnel. The malarial control unit, although functioning, has not controlled the rampant spread of malaria. People need advice on irrigated agriculture—they are misusing water supplies and salinating their land. Almost every kind of service that resettlers require is scarce.

Participation by resettlers was lacking until recently. People were inadequately consulted, and resettlement decisions did not conform to their needs or desires. This led to much greater resettler dissatisfaction than necessary. It also contributed to resettler dependency and a fatalistic attitude. People in resettlement villages strongly prefer to rely on the resettlement authorities rather than the Zilla Panchayat system of normal villages. At some point the special treatment will end and the resettlers themselves will have to be responsible for operation and maintenance.

NGOs probably could have contributed far more than they have. Useful in organizing people and promoting self-sufficiency, they could have used their experience to initiate more income-generating activities. The state government's negative attitude toward some advocacy NGOs has obscured its view of the positive potential that grassroots, field-based NGOs have for this kind of work. Only one of the chief secretaries supported NGO involvement, and when he was replaced, support for NGO involvement declined considerably. On the positive side, the Bank and the state government learned what it takes to turn a project around. Institutional strengthening, from the top position on down, was critical. After years of unprofessional management, the government now has a fully functioning management information system. Realistic budgeting and scheduling are at least feasible. The consent awards are a useful innovation in reducing the amount of wasted time, effort, and money in resolving complaints about compensation levels. This project has moved farther from confrontation to cooperation than many resettlement operations. However, it still has a long way to go.

Notes

1. All data in this and the following sections refer to the 1991, 1993, and 1997 survey samples, not the entire population affected by Narayanpur, unless specifically stated otherwise.
2. Because the 1993 survey did not include the unaffected villages, it is not possible to determine if the 20 percent decline took place at the same time, 1991 to 1993, as it did in the resettlement villages. However, the equal decline for both resettlement and unaffected villages is striking.

3

Commitment to Income
Recovery in China

Two China dam experiences, Shuikou and Yantan, demonstrate how sound resettlement practices led to successful and relatively rapid income restoration for affected households, even though large numbers of people had to be moved to terrain much less hospitable for farming than the areas they left.

Both dams filled up river valleys surrounded by steep hills, forcing most resettlers to forsake traditional paddy farming for intensive farm crops, tree crops, and nonfarm employment. In some cases, especially in Yantan, families had to migrate to other areas to be assured jobs. However, despite the lifestyle change this required, most households have seen their incomes increase substantially. Housing and services are better than before, and resettlers, especially in Shuikou, express satisfaction with their situations. Shuikou families' economic improvement was boosted by strong regional growth, a situation that did not apply to the more isolated Yantan. Nonetheless, in both areas most resettled households restored and increased family incomes surprisingly quickly.

This was in large part the result of a clear government mandate at both the national and local levels to ensure social welfare of the displaced families. This is reflected in:

- Comprehensive planning with extensive local government participation before dam construction even began.
- Involvement of all affected families in the decisions surrounding their relocation and employment.
- A continuing commitment by government to create jobs as the best means of ensuring income restoration.
- An unusual flexibility to modify strategies to cope with planning and budget deficiencies.

TABLE 3.1
Shuikou Project Chronology

Date	Event
1982–83	A resettlement plan is developed after extensive consultation with township and village leaders.
1984	The resettlement plan is approved.
1986	The dam project is approved.
1986	Shuikou Reservoir Resettlement Office is established to manage the resettlement project.
1987	Dam construction starts.
1988	Relocation starts.
1990–92	70 percent of affected population is moved.
1993	The reservoir is filled—all remaining resettlers are moved.
1994	Average household incomes pass predam levels.
2004	Shuikou Reservoir Resettlement Office (SRRO) is to remain engaged in recovery until this year.

Relocating 20,000 Families Successfully in a Challenging Rural Area

Of the two dam projects described here, Shuikou near the coast in the Fujian province is the main case. The Shuikou project was approved in 1987 and completed in 1997. It provided energy on schedule to support the rapid industrialization of the Fujian coastal economy. The World Bank identified the resettlement component in the early 1990s as a best-practice example of properly planned and executed involuntary resettlement. The Yantan project is a comparator, to see if the findings at Shuikou have relevance elsewhere in China. The project began in 1986 and reached completion in 1994 (table 3.1). Reports on the resettlement component suggest that the operation was less impressive than at Shuikou and that recovery to income and employment targets was delayed.

The two projects are similar in many ways. Both dams are in narrow valleys surrounded by hills and have reservoirs about 100 kilometers long. The powerhouses at Shuikou and Yantan have installed capacities of 1,400 and 1,100 megawatts. The projects, approved less than a year apart, have been critical in supplying energy fueling the development of their respective provinces, Fujian and Guangxi, on the southeast coast of China.

The key difference is economic conditions between the two regions. Shuikou is on the Min Jiang River, whose valley has traditionally been one of the richest parts of the province, supplying rice, fruit, and fish. Guangxi, especially the northwestern part where Yantan Dam is located, is much more mountainous, isolated, and therefore less developed. The objectives for both relocation programs were to move people short distances into comparable occupations. However, physical conditions and the isolation of the Yantan area greatly affected the resettlement and income restoration options.

Flooding the Narrow Valley Meant New Settlements and
New Occupations for Most Displacees

The dam and powerhouse[1] are 84 kilometers above the provincial capital near the coast. The reservoir extends another 96 kilometers up to and curving around the city of Nanping (map IBRD 30508). Altogether, 15,600 rural households with 67,200 people had to be moved. Another 20,000 urban people were relocated, including 3,900 households with 17,200 people in Nanping City. Living and cropping conditions in the four affected counties vary, but none have prime cultivable land.

Given the narrowness and steep sides of the valley, the only way to avoid moving people very far was to reestablish resettlement villages on newly created terraces and leveled hilltops. The almost total loss of level ground in the valley floor necessitated an income-restoration strategy tailored to the remaining natural resources. Most people were employed through a combination of:

- Orchards and tree farming on hillsides too steep for plowing
- Intensive farm activities, such as backyard mushroom growing, duck and pig farms, and fish and pearl ponds
- Service activities, such as shops and transport
- Small and medium-scale enterprises
- Migration, especially by persons with special skills.

One of the features of this program was to consolidate smaller villages in new towns wherever possible—if the residents agreed (map IBRD 30509). This led to the expansion of commercial enterprise and the profusion of open-ended, ground-floor shops stretching all along the central streets of the new towns. Most villages near the dam lost all lands and houses; new villages, towns, and occupations had to be constructed. Nearer the upstream end of the reservoir, for those villages that did not lose all their homes and lands, the displaced families would leapfrog to higher house sites. Among 89 affected villages, 73 required relocation of households; of these, 46 had to be completely rebuilt (or relocated to towns). The prevailing pattern of resettlement activity, however, was to rebuild, mostly on flattened hilltops and terraces.

Local governments played a vital part in the resettlement. Lee Travers, in his comprehensive 1993 review, *China—Involuntary Resettlement*, describes the historical factors that equipped these local governments to guide and carry out the planning and implementation of the Shuikou (and Yantan) resettlement program:

Successful resettlement requires management of major social change. Local governments in China have a long history of using planning tools to manage discontinuous change. Through participation in political and economic campaigns, county and township governments have experience in reallocating land, moving people, making new social and production investments, helping the

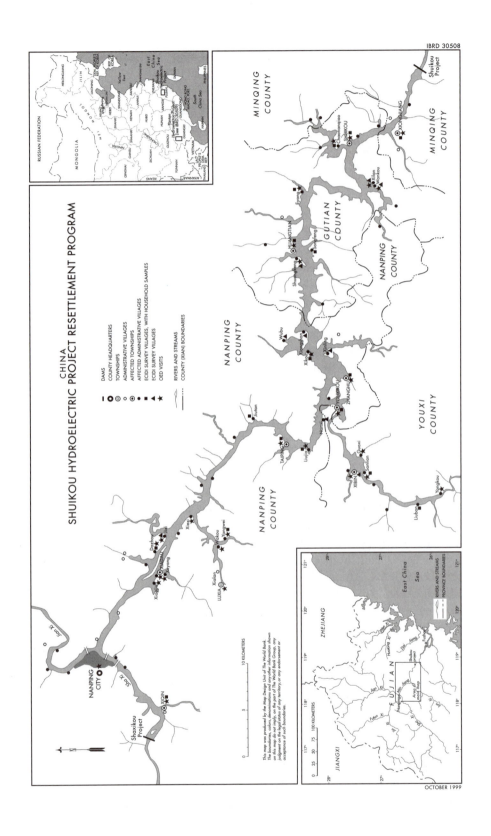

CHINA
SHUIKOU HYDROELECTRIC PROJECT RESETTLEMENT PROGRAM

IBRD 30508

DAMS
COUNTY HEADQUARTERS
TOWNSHIPS
ADMINISTRATIVE VILLAGES
AFFECTED TOWNSHIPS
AFFECTED ADMINISTRATIVE VILLAGES
ECIDI SURVEY VILLAGES
ECIDI SURVEY VILLAGES, WITH HOUSEHOLD SAMPLES
OED VISITS

RIVERS AND STREAMS
COUNTY (XIAN) BOUNDARIES

This map was produced by the Map Design Unit of The World Bank.
The boundaries, colors, denominations and any other information shown
on this map do not imply, on the part of The World Bank Group, any
judgment on the legal status of any territory, or any endorsement or
acceptance of such boundaries.

OCTOBER 1999

IBRD 30509

CHINA
YANTAN HYDROELECTRIC PROJECT RESETTLEMENT PROGRAM

— DAMS
◉ COUNTY HEADQUARTERS
◎ TOWNSHIPS
○ ADMINISTRATIVE VILLAGES
◉ AFFECTED TOWNSHIPS
● AFFECTED ADMINISTRATIVE VILLAGES
★ OED VISITS

RIVERS AND STREAMS
COUNTY (XIAN) BOUNDARIES

0   5   10   15 KILOMETERS

This map was produced by the Map Design Unit of The World Bank.
The boundaries, colors, denominations and any other information shown
on this map do not imply, on the part of The World Bank Group, any
judgment on the legal status of any territory, or any endorsement or
acceptance of such boundaries.

TIANÉ

TIANÉ
COUNTY

LUOFU
NANDAN

BANMO

NANDAN
COUNTY

JINGU

N

Laji
Hydropower
Station

CHANGJIANG

AIDONG

DONGLAN
CHANGLE

DONGLAN
COUNTY

DATONG

SANSHI

BANSHEN

RELOCATION OUTSIDE RESERVOIR AREA

106°   108°   110°   112°
26°

GUIZHOU   To Duyun   To Hengyang

HUNAN

Longtan
Dam

To Anshun   Donglan   Guilin

Bama

Yantan Dam   Long Jiang   Luzhai

Etan
Dam   Liuzhou

See main map
for detail   Dahua   Hexian
Dam

Lin Jiang

24°   G U A N G X I   Xun Jiang   24°

Bingyang   Litang Farm   Wuzhou

Yong   Guigang   Xi Jiang
Jiang   Yu

Nanning   GUANGDONG

22°   22°

Qinzhou   Shapokou Farm
Xin Xin Farm

Pingxiang

VIETNAM   Fangcheng
Beihai   Zhanjiang

Gulf of Tonkin

0   50   100   150 KILOMETERS

106°   108°   110°

RESETTLEMENT
FARMS
MAIN ROADS
PROVINCE
BOUNDARIES
INTERNATIONAL
BOUNDARIES

RUSSIAN FEDERATION

HEILONGJIANG

MONGOLIA

JILIN

NEI   LIAONING   DEM. PEOPLE'S
MONGOL   REP. OF KOREA

BEIJING SHI   TIANJIN SHI   REP. OF
HEBEI   KOREA

SHANXI   SHANDONG

QINGHAI   GANSU   Yellow
Sea

SHAANXI   HENAN   JIANGSU

ANHUI   SHANGHAI SHI

XIZANG   HUBEI   East
China
ZHEJIANG   Sea

SICHUAN   Shuikou
Hydroelectric
HUNAN   JIANGXI   Project
(see IBRD 30508)

GUIZHOU   FUJIAN   TAIWAN
Yantan
Hydroelectric
Project

YUNNAN   GUANGDONG
GUANGXI   HONG KONG
MACAO, PORT.

MYANMAR   VIETNAM
LAO   HAINAN   South
PEOPLE'S   China Sea
DEM.   PHILIPPINES
THAILAND   REP.

Pangzhongtang
Hydropower
Station   DONGSHAN

FENGHUANG

Cifu
Hydropower
Station

BAMA   Cifu   BAIJING   Nase

Napa   Shanjiao

BAMA
COUNTY

Yixu

Changji   DAHUA
COUNTY

NATAO   Yantan
Project

JIANGXU   DUYANG

OCTOBER 1999

labor market to absorb new entrants, and other key elements of a major resettlement effort. When those actions took place with scant regard for individual welfare, as they did at times during the Great Leap Forward and Cultural Revolution, they inflicted great harm, but the record in the last decade shows how well the tools can work when applied to the goal of maintaining well being.[2]

Implementing Resettlement Requires Flexibility

In implementing resettlement, the best-laid plans oft go awry. Flexibility is key.

Relocation Is On Time, but Infrastructure for Economic Rehabilitation Falls Behind

Although the dam project did not begin until 1987, by 1985 the outline of the resettlement plan had been established on the basis of national policies and regulations on involuntary resettlement issued in the early 1980s. The Shuikou resettlement planning process required extensive consultation with township and village leaders, particularly in selecting resettlement sites and identifying the major economic rehabilitation options. The four counties drafted the plans for their jurisdictions. The overall plan was approved by the provincial government in 1983 and by the national government the next year.

In 1986, the provincial government established the SRRO to manage the resettlement component. Although physical relocation was to be preceded by investments establishing new production systems for groups or individuals well before their move, this scheduling strategy broke down. Facing annual shortfalls in funding, SRRO and the local governments concentrated on completing the relocation of infrastructure—roads, site leveling, water supplies—at the expense of the development budget.[3] Thus, less than half the fruit trees were planted before 1990—only three years before the reservoir was filled.[4]

Construction started in 1987. Relocation took place over a six year period, beginning in 1988, with almost 70 percent of the population moved in the period 1990–92. In addition to the relocation of 67,200 rural people from the valley floor, another 17,200 people resident in Nanping had to be moved to make way for the construction of embankments and a renewal of waterfront property. Most of those people were placed in ten large apartment buildings, sited at varying distances from the city center on the waterfront. Families paid one-third the capital costs of the new apartments, a contribution that substantially understated the improvement in conditions (including provision of utilities) that the majority of urban displacees now enjoyed. Most of these displacees maintained their old jobs.

Job Creation Is the Road to Income Recovery.

Incomes and Jobs. The principal distinguishing feature of the Shuikou (and Yantan) experience is the continuing commitment to income targets as a component of resettlement objectives. When the original plans for creating new income bases were frustrated, the authorities shifted to other strategies. The driving force has been a concern for employment targets rather than income targets. SRRO and all associates in the lower-level administrative offices involved with the post-relocation stages of resettlement have aimed first at a target called "arranged jobs," which the Chinese define as a productive and reliable source of wage or other cash income from an organized occupation.

Using the number of employable individuals in the towns and villages, SRRO sought to arrange a job for each individual. In fact, local governments throughout China are preoccupied with this task. Town and village authorities ensured wherever possible that each family had at least one reliable job before other families got two jobs. Isolated households could of course miss out on that equitable solution.

Restoration of "incomes" and "living standards" is an important element of national and provincial resettlement policy; however, the Chinese position is that by managing employment they can also deliver on incomes. The most desirable arranged jobs are permanent positions in, for example, an official township office or a factory. In agriculture, arranged jobs are measured by units of land dedicated to a cash crop. If the village authority assigns a displaced family to paddy, citrus, or timber holdings of those sizes, or a combination of smaller holdings, it can assert that it has arranged a job. The spontaneous cultivation of subsistence crops on "wasteland" does not count. Most of the persons who did not have arranged jobs were busy doing these unorganized jobs and may have even been receiving substantial incomes from them. The authorities know these individuals. If the authorities are able to attract a new industry to the village, the jobs created are (in principle) offered to these individuals first.

Income Strategies. The process of arranging jobs went through two phases. The first phase was aimed at land-based employment. Of all jobs to be created, 74 percent were to be in recognized agricultural occupations: paddy and other grain crops, fruit trees, other economic trees (such as tea, tung oil, and bamboo), and commercial forestry. One key target was the development of approximately 2,000 hectares of new plowable lands for grains and vegetables to replace the same amount of flooded paddy land.

The other job categories available to the planners have been grouped as:

- Intensive "sideline" farm activities, such as cultivating backyard mushrooms, raising ducks and pigs, and managing fish ponds and oyster (pearl) beds
- Service activities, such as shops, restaurants, and transport
- Industrial activities, large—and small-scale
- Migration.

These four groups of jobs were included in the first phase, although not emphasized.

The assignment of individuals to jobs appears to have been a thoroughly participative process. Families and individuals were asked to choose among already identified or projected opportunities. The rules on a minimum-size economic holding had to be respected. The process by which the cultivable land was allocated when there were more families asking for it than could be arranged varied from village to village. However, it appears that through a lottery or another transparent and acceptable formula, competition and favoritism were avoided. Families were asked to select among completely new life-styles, for example, the paddy-farming family that opts for fish cages [5] or tangerines.

The land-based strategy succeeded for the tree and forestry sectors, but failed to provide the cultivable land for field crops. By project completion, only 700 hectares of plowable land had been developed (compared with 2,100 projected).[6] The amount of cultivable farmland per capita for resettlers had fallen. Most of that land was inferior to the bottomland that had been lost. As a result, the authorities had to arrange many more off-farm jobs than expected.

This is where the real success at Shuikou emerges: the adjustment away from traditional agriculture. The leading edge was provided by the town and village enterprises that sprung up everywhere. The creation of most of the infrastructure for these enterprises was financed from town and village resources, individual savings, and outside (including foreign) sources. Ownership took many forms—local government, individuals, and joint ventures[7]—although public owners usually contracted private individuals to manage the business. The other opening was through migration. Certain communities in the Shuikou area had long been noted for particular skills: asbestos insulation and amusement park construction, for example. The rapid growth of the Chinese economy spurred the demand for these and other services, prompting increasing numbers of members of those communities to leave for temporary assignments.

Acceleration of economic activity along the lakeside corridor to Nanping was part of a regional phenomenon in Fujian Province and elsewhere along the Chinese coast, fueled by funds from Taiwan and Hong Kong. Thus, the Shuikou "success" was helped by major structural changes that provided jobs and markets for the displacees. However, the exertions of local authorities in pushing along this process were substantial, and for many towns and villages decisive.

That explains another distinctive feature at Shuikou: the variability in economic performance of the local administrations. Some were more adept than others at attracting investments, facilitating migration, and arranging for technical assistance for persons embarking in new occupations. As a rule, however, all governments were committed to making resettlement work, and in any jurisdiction significantly affected by the dam, government took recovery as the most important single objective of its administration.

Total Costs Are Not Available

The total costs of Shuikou resettlement are not available. Expenditures through 1996 were Y1,092 million, or about $200 million at applicable exchange rates. SRRO estimates that contributions by county, township, and local governments would have equaled those components of the official resettlement budget channeled through SRRO for investments in infrastructure. Besides these investments in site infrastructure and land preparation, there are the additional costs to resettlers of house building and, of much greater importance, the substantial second-phase investments in town and village enterprise from public and private sources. For a very rough estimate of the specific costs of Shuikou resettlement per family, one can double the $200 million figure and divide by the 17,000 relocated families. That results in a figure of about $24,000 per family.

Compensation at Shuikou Is a Combination of Cash and Economic Infrastructure

At Shuikou, the key objectives were to provide adequate compensation for all lost production and household assets, to restore the productive base and income levels, and to accomplish these objectives giving priority to land-based employment arrangements, to moving minimum distances, and to retaining the existing village social and administrative structures. The state encouraged "developmental" resettlement, meaning that it should focus more on the productive base than on "passive" compensation. China's land tenure system, wherein all productive land assets are collectively owned, was well suited to this approach.

SRRO compensated individual families for flooded homes, fruit trees, and other assets on each household's home plot. Compensation for the houses reflected actual values, less salvageable materials, plus transport, and were made in cash or in access to new materials at subsidized prices or both. All households benefited from superior materials for rebuilding; many farmers contributed their own funds to enlarge the structures. Compensation to the families for other assets on their home plots could be in cash, but more often was packaged with the villages' developmental assistance for the same families. SRRO compensated the villages and townships for productive land, as well as for community infrastructure and other assets lost to the reservoir. This was the principal source for financing both the villages' collective economic recovery programs (such as leveling terraces for group orchards, and establishing local industry) and the incentive packages aimed at individual families. Families that lost farmland would be helped to develop new lands or to get established in other farm or nonfarm occupations. The system resulted in very little direct and unrestricted cash payoff.

Relocated households received a standard-size house plot with infrastructure. Plots in new towns and villages were assigned through a lottery. Households were responsible for constructing their new dwellings, except for "vulnerable" families—elderly, disabled, or others without able-bodied workers—for which the government contracted to build homes. Eligibility issues related to the family's claims on land did not arise because there was no private ownership.

Income Restoration Brings Higher Incomes, Better Living Conditions, and Resettler Satisfaction

1997 data show that resettler incomes have continued to increase. The restructuring of the income base has continued unabated, with land-based sources again receding. In one accounting, the traditional agricultural subsectors—projected in the original plans to provide 74 percent of the jobs—have shrunk in importance to a 26 percent share.[8] In another accounting, the town and village enterprises and other nonfarm occupations contributed to 75 percent of the increase in overall incomes between 1995 and 1996.[9] The nonfarm categories of services, industry, and migration now provide 65 percent of all arranged jobs and, because incomes are higher in these categories, a larger share of total arranged income.

The data show that control group incomes exceed the resettler incomes, but the latter are slowly closing the gap. Since 1993, when all the resettlers moved, their average incomes have increased at a rate 17 percent faster than the control group. They are likely to close the gap more rapidly in future, since the resettlers' occupational structure was forced to shift more rapidly to the fastest-growing components of the economy. Survey data show that relocated families tend to have more living space and own more assets (bicycles, sewing machines, and electrical appliances) than before.

Another welcome trend is a shift to more equitable income distribution among the resettlers. That is supported by additional information on the recovery of households in the lowest income group. Of 15 families identified as among the poorest in the sample of 524 households, per capita income increased 55 percent from 1995 to 1996.

Responsibility for rebuilding social infrastructure rested with local governments. In addition to the compensation received for the demolished structures, these entities provided their own resources to rebuild. Newly constructed community centers were almost always of better quality. In one township, the number of elementary schools fell from 34 to 28, reflecting the process of consolidation, but floor space increased 43 percent. The numbers of middle schools and clinics remained the same. Water supply and electricity indicators increased, while the road system was extended. The telephone growth rate has been explosive. These trends would be representative of all the reconstructed sites: radical improvement in construction materials, coupled with growth in the number of some categories of facilities, and an expansion of utilities.

In the course of this study, many families and individuals were asked about their satisfaction with the resettlement; the answers were invariably positive. The respondents could distinguish the valued components of their previous condition that were lost forever, and the advantages of the new lifestyles, and weigh the two. However, it was impossible to determine how much of the present high level of satisfaction was attributable to intelligent management of relocation and recovery and how much to the fortuitous expansion of the Fujian economy.

Government Performance Shows Commitment, Flexibility, and a Vision of Development

China's strong commitment and successful management of this program results from its view of resettlement not as a burden, but as an opportunity to pursue economic growth. Resettlement is implicitly approached as *a development opportunity*, as resettlement funds are used to improve existing lands, make marginal lands fit for agriculture, to expand the area of irrigation, to establish new enterprises, or to expand the scope of existing enterprises.

An important facet of Chinese commitment is the flexibility authorities showed in the shift to the second phase of development activities. More recently, the emergence of a third phase can even be detected: remedial actions taken by local officials to rescue, reorient, or replace failing activities initiated earlier. Up to now, however, the authorities have been more involved in rescuing failing agricultural enterprises: citrus orchards, for example, where the original selection of species proved inappropriate for the area and it was necessary to shift to other citrus species, longan, olive, or some other tree crop. For the future, SRRO intends to abandon the weaker town and village enterprises, especially the collectively owned ones, and press for industrial activities fully structured to meet the tests of the free market. In addition, SRRO has agreed to continue operation until 2004, to ensure that income restoration is completed. Although there is an evident willingness to maintain the momentum of development at Shuikou, this third phase of government interventions is still in its infancy. SRRO does not yet have firm and sustainable institutional support.

The record is not uniformly favorable. Chinese performance at Shuikou clearly could have been improved. Budget shortfalls at the center, aggravated by budget practices that do not anticipate inflation, and SRRO's decision to complete the relocation program first, delayed the development activities in particular.

Local Government and Villagers Participate in Making Decisions about Villagers' Futures

During the early planning period, when large-scale maps were drawn indicating preferred sites of the new towns and villages and the availability of unused land for development, the resettlement planning team dealt exclusively with the town and village leaders. By involving the village leaders, the authorities were drawing the individual households into the planning framework, but indirectly. In the next stage, however, the households were brought into the center of the process. This fully participatory approach is unavoidable, given the land tenure system and the provision of funds for land compensation to the local authorities.

These propitious factors compelled local governments to engage in detailed discussion with each family, to determine a plan specific to each and make an appropriate allocation of village developmental funds. Since families could not claim compensation for the land they farmed, or expect equal allocations of farmland to everyone in the new deal, they were powerless to reconstruct their lives without local government support. However, these families could choose their own postdam occupations, within limits set by fund availability and the natural resource base. It was the job of the local authorities to guide each family to a promising plan. Once approved, these individual family plans determined overall allocations, integration with families of similar preferences, and types of technical assistance required.

Resettler participation extended to some macro-level decisions about relocation. Families and their local officials met to discuss proposed sites for the new villages and the merits of combining with other villages and towns. In one small lakeside village, families had been dislodged by the highway (not the lake) and had voted against integrating with a new town five kilometers away. An area in the town had been set aside for them, but they preferred to remain apart, and the authorities respected that preference. That town itself became famous later when, as an afterthought, the townspeople voted to overrule the original plan to move the whole town back and requested that a kilometer-long embankment be built to protect the old center. This request was also honored.

A Good National Policy on Involuntary Resettlement
Continues to Improve

The basic pieces of central government policy and regulatory provisions on involuntary resettlement had been established by the time Shuikou was appraised, in a cascade of circulars from 1982 to 1985. Since then, the Chinese have continued to improve the resettlement package. For example, the compensation package for the Ertan resettlement program is better than at Shuikou, and the average budget allocations per household have almost tripled.

One improvement in national policy on resettlement that will positively affect Shuikou and all other schemes is advanced in a State Planning Commission circular issued in 1996, creating a "later stage support fund." The circular provides for a substantial increase in the fraction of annual revenues from power generation that has to be turned over to provincial governments for operation, maintenance, and further development of resettlement schemes behind large- and medium-size hydroelectric dams. Provincial authorities are expected to decide how to divide that windfall addition between maintenance of resettlement infrastructure and further developmental works. The Bank estimates that about $2.5 million will be available annually from this source, replacing the official Shuikou resettlement budget, which is now exhausted.

TABLE 3.2
Summary Comparison—Shuikou and Yantan

Aspect	Shuikou	Yantan
Location	Near coast in Fujian province, in narrow river valley requiring that resettlers move to steep hills	In interior of Guangxi region, with similar but steeper topography than Shuikou
Regional economy	Rapidly developing	Isolated—not near large cities or coastal areas where development is occurring
Number displaced	20,100 households, comprising 87,200 people	8,900 households, comprising 43,200 people
Resettlement strategy	Resettle close to original settlement in similar occupations, consolidate villages, and develop small businesses, intensive farm activities and services; encourage migration when appropriate.	Same, but after initial stages, much greater emphasis on migration
Problems	Budget shortfalls delayed job preparation (for example, tree planting); farm employment possibilities greatly overestimated.	Same
Results	With increased emphasis on nonfarm occupations, most resettlers have arranged jobs, although figures are not provided. Resettler incomes are increasing and now exceed control group.	Despite the government's encouraging substantial migration, by 1997 8,000 out of the 25,000–strong labor force were without arranged jobs. Many of them work in informal sector. Incomes are rising, although settlers rely on a grain subsidy to supplement income.

In Yantan, the Same Principles Are Applied under Harsher Conditions

In Yantan, the principles applied to the project were similar to those applied in Shuikou (table 3.2). The Yantan Hydroelectric Project constructed a 110–meter-high, concrete, gravity dam on the Hongshui River in the Guangxi autonomous region (map IBRD 30509); four generating units totaling 1,210 megawatts, and transmission lines to connect the station to the South China grid and the cities of the coast. The government's detailed resettlement plan provided for relocation and reestablishment of living standards for all project-affected persons. The State Planning Commission had approved the resettlement plan in 1983, two years ahead of Shuikou, and used the same intensive village-level analysis of resources and labor supply.

The guiding principles of resettlement were also the same—to move people short distances and into occupations comparable to those abandoned. Yantan faced the same disadvantage as Shuikou: to stay close to the reservoir the people were forced up the hills and ridges onto land poorly suited to producing grain crops. However, in the Yantan case, the topography is steeper. In addition, the options outside agriculture are more limited. Yantan is far from the major urban centers of Guangxi and farther still from the booming coastal economy. The average income level in Guangxi was about three-quarters that of the Fujian Province in the mid-1980s, and the gap has widened.

Implementation Shows Flexibility

Ninety-six percent of the households that had to move—all of those threatened—were relocated by the time the gates were closed to fill the reservoir in March 1992. The dam and reservoir ultimately affected 62,400 people, of whom 43,200 people in 7,000 households had to be moved. As at Shuikou, the availability of cultivable land was overestimated. The principal agriculture activities of the resettlers are fruit, forestry, and other tree crops. New industrial enterprises absorbed a small fraction of the labor force. County, township, and village officials again were active in identifying possibilities and persuading and assisting families to take them up.

Households struggled to manage a range of new activities. One former paddy farm family, for example, was grouped with five others in operating a fish pen in a small cove, while growing sugar cane and cassava on 1/15 hectare each (one mu) and caring for a 1/2 hectare (seven mu) of a fir plantation halfway through its ten year growth to maturity and harvesting.

Of the 25,000 persons in the labor force, 17,000 had arranged jobs by March 1997—five years after the reservoir was filled. Many of the remainder were engaged in subsistence activities—cultivating cassava and maize on the hillsides—that are not counted in official statistics. However, the provincial government recognized from the beginning that a large number cannot be brought on to the official lists through placement in local farm and nonfarm jobs. As an alternative, it has engaged in the organized transfer of excess people from the most vulnerable villages and townships to other parts of Guangxi. In 1992, 3,600 people (representing 1,000 arranged jobs) were transported to two sugar estates. In 1997, 11,500 people (representing 3,000 arranged jobs) moved to the site of another government-owned farm in Binyang County (map IBRD 30509). Including both Bei Hai and Binyang, the province moved almost 25 percent of those affected out of the valley.

With Income Restoration, Average Income Rise, but Settlers Rely on Grain Subsidy

Compensation practices resembled those at Shuikou. On this scheme, most of the packages offered to the families were converted into loans, which they were to pay off on easy terms. Families that had lost more land were entitled to bigger loans, although the limiting factors were more often the size of the family and its interest in higher-cost enterprises. Yantan resettlement suffered the cost overruns experienced at Shuikou. Local governments again made large contributions.

Evidence suggests that present average income levels of resettlers in the three counties substantially exceed their predam incomes—more than double in two of the counties. Thus, the project has succeeded in restoring the standard of living, albeit with radically different lifestyles for most resettlers. Resettler incomes, however, are below the incomes of unaffected people in the same jurisdictions, and that gap has been widening, because of the lag time in establishing the new enterprises and bringing them to maturity (especially the orchards and other trees). The averages for both resettlers and unaffected people are still far below averages in the rapidly developing regions of China, including Shuikou, and below even the poverty thresholds established for Guangxi.

All persons significantly affected by the dam, except the Bei Hai migrants, receive a monthly food grain ration of 150 kilograms per capita per year, or 800 kilograms for the average family of just over five persons. It is insufficient to sustain the adult farm worker (250 kilometers per capita is considered the threshold) but provides a reliable basis for the family economy.

Asked about their satisfaction, resettlers typically lamented the loss of the easily farmed valley paddy land but accepted that the new farm enterprises promised good returns in the future. Those families that had shifted out of agriculture and acquired urban status welcomed the security of fixed, off-farm income. However, it was clear that the monthly grain ration figured largely in this appraisal. The houses are invariably better, at least in structure and material, and usually in size. Almost all houses—except for the most isolated—are hooked up to electricity and have running water.

Conclusions

China's performance in these two projects is impressive. When funding shortfalls and delays in execution upset the implementation schedule for relocating households, the executing agencies were determined to catch up and invariably did so. The implementation record on developmental activities aimed at recovery of incomes is less satisfactory, although the level of commitment to reaching successful outcomes in employment and welfare is unmistakable. The emphasis on jobs and incomes, and the thoroughly participative process whereby households and local government authorities are brought into planning and implementation, represent "best practices" for involuntary resettlement efforts.

The most impressive aspect of this story for the current study is that China takes income restoration and development as seriously as physical relocation. China and the provincial governments grasp forced resettlement as an opportunity for promoting regional development. The impression is enhanced by the high standards China sets for the minimum conditions on the jobs it is trying to create. It is aiming to provide secure bases for family income and welfare. China does not consider some traditional occupations—such as rainfed farming for subsistence—as acceptable outcomes.

China's evident concern for jobs, incomes, full participation, family welfare, and equitable growth—at least as demonstrated on these two schemes—illuminates the ongoing debate over Chinese respect for human rights. It supports government's assertion that whatever its attitude toward freedom of political expression, its recent record on furthering the ideals of family welfare must be respected.[10]

The Shuikou incomes policy was pushed along handsomely by the rapid industrialization of the southeastern Chinese coast, but the contributions went both ways. SRRO's programs provided the infrastructure and excess labor, and the dam provided cheap electricity to keep that dynamic process moving.

Yantan's progress in job recreation and income restoration has been slower. However, the Yantan authorities did something the Shuikou authorities did not have to do: organize the migration of workers to areas with excess cultivable land. At both schemes, spontaneous migration by individual workers also helped to broaden the income base. Promoting organized and spontaneous migration to strengthen an income policy for a resettlement scheme is a creative solution when there are remunerative employment opportunities within the reach of the migrants.

In many ways China is unique. The persistence of planning, coupled with collective ownership of rural land and other resources, and the importance of local government in shaping investment are advantages impossible to export. Nevertheless, at least four ingredients in the China recipe can be used elsewhere.

- The idea of approaching involuntary resettlement as a developmental opportunity and marshaling a range of instruments to carry it out.
- An imaginative exploration of micro-opportunities, propelled by the conviction that any but the most hostile environments offer a multitude of options. The ability to force the expansion of fish farming from cages and pens, of pearl culture from these and similar pens, of stone cutting, of exotic fruits when the traditional ones fail, and, even, of polished golf club heads, is an acquired skill, not unique to the Chinese.
- The flexibility to adjust strategies when early ones break down, shifting to other sets of employment opportunities if necessary or stepping back in to rehabilitate/restructure failing enterprises.
- The crucial involvement of local governments, especially the elected leaders. The objective is not only to secure their ownership, but also to "wed their interests to those of local residents."

Notes

1. The dam is a concrete gravity dam that is 101 meters high and 786 meters long. Its reservoir, at a full operating level of 65 meters, has a surface area of 300 square kilometers. The powerhouse has a generating capacity of 1,400 megawatts, with seven units of 200 megawatts each.

2. Travers, *China—Involuntary Resettlement*, p. 18–19. Travers' historical sections illuminate present practice. He points to the magnitude of forced resettlement in China in recent decades: 32 million people moved in the past 40 years, 10 million of them from reservoirs and the rest to make way for investments in transportation, industry, and urban redevelopment. He also describes the difficult period in the 1960s and 1970s, when, notwithstanding regulations favoring resettlers issued in the early 1950s, the government's attitude changed and the onus of recovery and even survival was passed to the resettlers. The mottoes were self-reliance and sacrifice, in the interests of the state. He estimates that two-thirds of the people resettled in that period failed to recover their former standards of living, half of them ending up at subsistence levels and the other half in abject poverty. The policy reforms of the early 1980s were in fact a return to policies adopted 30 years before.

3. SRRO refers to this budget as the "compensation" budget, since the objectives of compensation and development are fused.

4. Since most of the farmers had access to their old fields until 1993, the critical income gap, for the new fruit farmers, for example, was between 1993 and the first fruit harvests, which were five to eight years after planting.

5. The development of fish-cage farming at Shuikou is worth a report of its own. China produces about half the world's catch from aquaculture and is the leader also in the use of cages. The Shuikou valley farmers had little experience with this practice, but it caught on quickly in several locations. Xongjiang township officials reported growth in the number of cages from eight in 1992 to 1,026 in 1996, with plans for expansion to 1,500 in 1997. The fishery sector at the Shuikou reservoir was written up in a consultant's report to the Bank (F. Lin, 1992, *Experiences in Chinese Reservoir Fisheries and Aspects of Planning for Reservoir Fisheries in the Shuikou Hydroelectric Project*, Iowa Institute of Hydraulic Research, University of Iowa, Iowa City).

6. Since 1995 some townships have been expanding this perimeter.

7. One example: the 46 town and village enterprises established in Xibin Township were divided into ten enterprises that were owned by villages, 18 private ventures owned by four townships, and 14 joint ventures between villages and townships.

8. From ECIDI's 1997 village survey.

9. From ECIDI's analysis of 1997 data from a subset of 5 villages.

10. Again, Travers, in *China-Involuntary Resettlement* (p. 12), speaks to this point: "the current Chinese system far outperforms those in most of the developing countries in protecting the interests of resettlement communities."

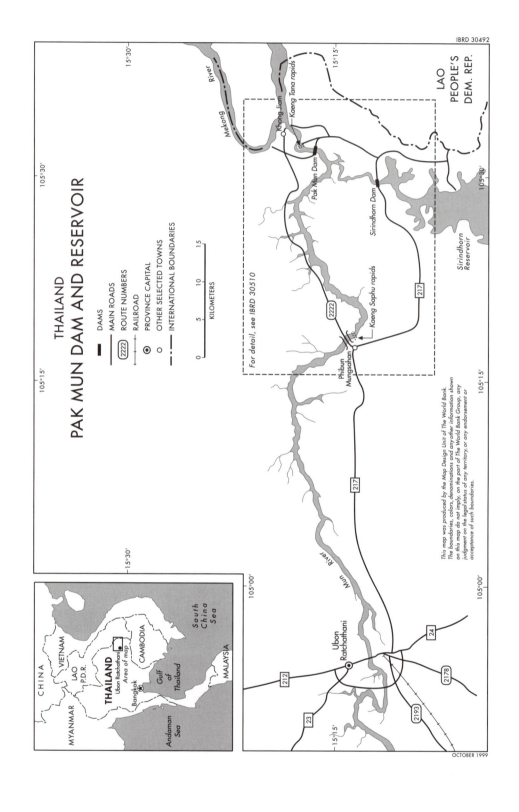

THAILAND
PAK MUN DAM AND RESERVOIR

DAMS
MAIN ROADS
2222 ROUTE NUMBERS
RAILROAD
⊛ PROVINCE CAPITAL
○ OTHER SELECTED TOWNS
INTERNATIONAL BOUNDARIES

KILOMETERS
0   5   10   15

For detail, see IBRD 30510

This map was produced by the Map Design Unit of The World Bank.
The boundaries, colors, denominations and any other information shown
on this map do not imply, on the part of The World Bank Group, any
judgment on the legal status of any territory, or any endorsement or
acceptance of such boundaries.

IBRD 30492

LAO
PEOPLE'S
DEM. REP.

Mekong River
Khong Jiam
Kaeng Tana rapids
Pak Mun Dam
Sirindhorn Dam
Sirindhorn Reservoir
Kaeng Saphu rapids
2222
217
Phibun Mungsahan
Mun River
217
Ubon Ratchathani
212
23
2193
2178
24

15°30'
15°15'
15°5'
15°00'
105°15'
105°30'
105°30'
105°15'
105°00'

CHINA
MYANMAR
VIETNAM
LAO P.D.R.
THAILAND
Ubon Ratchathani
Area of map
Bangkok
CAMBODIA
Gulf of Thailand
Andaman Sea
South China Sea
MALAYSIA

OCTOBER 1999

4

Responsiveness at High Cost in Thailand

Pak Mun illustrates the issues that can arise in determining fair compensation for people affected by dam construction. Already facing scrutiny by environmental NGOs that opposed large dam construction, Thailand's Electrical Generating Authority (EGAT) made their best effort to minimize adverse impacts of the dam and to establish equitable compensation. However, early mistakes left EGAT embroiled in controversy. First, they neglected to collect baseline data just before resettlement to assess incomes and land prices of the affected households. Without this information, they had little basis to refute the resettlers' demands. Second, communication with the villagers was poor during the first years of dam construction, leaving much misunderstanding and distrust about the impacts of the dam. Related to this, the government established its early relocation plans on the basis of assumptions that hadn't been discussed with the involved families. These assumptions proved false and added to the villagers' grievances. Third, the government failed to recognize that increased pressures on available land would raise land prices, affecting the adequacy of compensation packages developed only a few years earlier.

NGOs found willing partners in the disgruntled villagers to protest compensation and resettlement plans. However, Pak Mun was a relatively small project involving limited resettlement. While it was in the government's interest to accommodate the settlers to keep the project on schedule, the government's willingness to negotiate may have contributed to successive demands for increasing compensation. Even so, the strategy succeeded. Relocation proceeded smoothly, but at a high cost.

With few exceptions, resettlers have done well in terms of both increased incomes and quality of life. This is mainly because of the growth that northeast Thailand was experiencing. It was helped along, however, by generous compensation and the opportunity for people to shift to nonfarm employment.

Amidst Controversy, Electric Authority Applies a High-Cost Solution to Negotiating Compensation

Pak Mun is located in northeast Thailand on the lower reaches of the Mun River, 5.5 kilometers above its confluence with the Mekong, which forms the border between Thailand and Laos (map IBRD 30492). Four years before dam construction began (in 1990), EGAT revised the dam's design to lower its height, greatly reducing the size of the reservoir and the number of inundated households.

EGAT's resettlement policy established land compensation rates above prevailing market prices. The generosity of the compensation may have contributed to the ensuing rapid inflation in land prices. NGOs organized resettlers to protest for higher rates, resulting in successive renegotiations of compensation. The result of increasingly generous compensation policies was to drive resettlement costs from $11.8 million to $19.7 million. However, this resulted in a remarkably smooth relocation and left the majority of resettlers better off than before the move. In fact, potential resettlers at other dam sites under consideration have asked to be treated as generously as Pak Mun resettlers.

Run-of-the-River Dam Construction Results in Minimal Land Loss and Relocation

Planning for the development of the Pak Mun Dam began in the 1960s. Environmental studies completed in January 1982 indicated that some 4,000 households would have to be relocated if the reservoir were impounded to a level of 113 meters above sea level (table 4.1). After extensive additional environmental studies, an alternative design for 108 meters was agreed upon in 1985. These adjustments cut power benefits and halved the reservoir length and surface area. The resulting resettlement population decreased from 20,000 people to about 1,500 people (241 households). EGAT, on its own without external pressure, had followed the first principle of sound resettlement policy: to minimize involuntary resettlement.

The final design was a 17 meter-high, concrete dam rising only five meters above the river banks, whose powerhouse provides 136 megawatts of peak-power generating capacity. The reservoir is about 40 kilometers long, with a surface area only marginally larger than the normal high-water level during the rainy season, when the river covers 44 square kilometers. Only nine square kilometers of agricultural land and seven square kilometers of secondary woodland were submerged.

The dam and reservoir affected 31 villages (map IBRD 30510). Altogether, about 1,700 households lost their homes, land, or both (including the 241 families whose homes and land were inundated as projected in the resettlement design, 671 whose homes were not inundated but who opted to relocate, and 780 who lost part of their land). Almost 6,000 households have claimed lost fishing

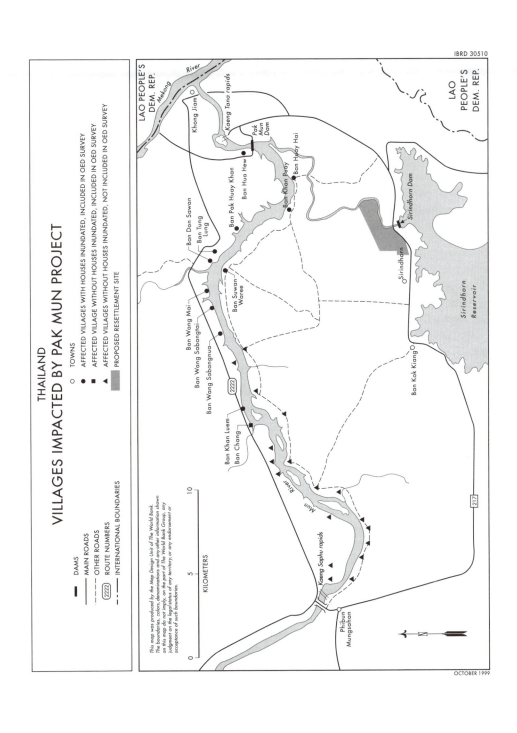

THAILAND

VILLAGES IMPACTED BY PAK MUN PROJECT

○ TOWNS

● AFFECTED VILLAGES WITH HOUSES INUNDATED, INCLUDED IN OED SURVEY

● AFFECTED VILLAGE WITHOUT HOUSES INUNDATED, INCLUDED IN OED SURVEY

■ AFFECTED VILLAGES WITHOUT HOUSES INUNDATED, INCLUDED IN OED SURVEY

▲ AFFECTED VILLAGES WITHOUT HOUSES INUNDATED, NOT INCLUDED IN OED SURVEY

▨ PROPOSED RESETTLEMENT SITE

━━ DAMS

──── MAIN ROADS

─ ─ ─ OTHER ROADS

(2222) ROUTE NUMBERS

─·─·─ INTERNATIONAL BOUNDARIES

This map was produced by the Map Design Unit of The World Bank.
The boundaries, colors, denominations and any other information shown
on this map do not imply, on the part of The World Bank Group, any
judgment on the legal status of any territory, or any endorsement or
acceptance of such boundaries.

KILOMETERS

0   5   10

IBRD 30510

OCTOBER 1999

LAO PEOPLE'S DEM. REP.

Mekong River

Khong Jiam

Kaeng Tana rapids

Pak Mun Dam

Ban Hua Hew

Ban Pak Huay Khan

Ban Don Sawan

Ban Tung Lung

Ban Suwan Waree

Ban Wang Mai

Ban Wang Sabangtai

Ban Wang Sabangnua

Ban Khan Luem

Ban Chang

Mun River

Kaeng Saphu rapids

Phibun Mungsahan

Ban Khan Pooy

Ban Huay Hai

Sirindhorn Dam

Sirindhorn

Sirindhorn Reservoir

Ban Kok Kiang

LAO PEOPLE'S DEM. REP.

217

2222

TABLE 4.1
Project Chronology

Date	Event
1982	The original dam design calls for relocation of 4,000 households.
1985	After environmental studies, an alternative design is approved that reduces reservoir length and surface area and decreases inundation to 241 households.
1990	Two committees are established to handle all resettlement issues. The base resettlement plan is completed, assuming households would move to resettlement area 15 kilometers distant.
1990	Dam construction begins.
1990	Resettlement begins.
1991	Farmers and NGOs protest compensation and resettlement terms.
1991	In response, EGAT quintuples compensation rates.
1993	Generous compensation leads to severe increase in land prices, spurring further settler protests.
1993	EGAT agrees that households could opt for nearby land rather than land at the resettlement site (which no one had accepted).
1994	EGAT offers compensation to families "inconvenienced" by dam construction.
1994, April	NGOs and villagers protest the dam's effect on fish catches.
1994, April	The dam is completed.
1994, Sept.	Relocation of households is completed.
1994	Government establishes committee that includes NGOs and affected people to determine fair compensation for fishing families, resulting in cash compensation and a cooperative development scheme.
1996	More settlers protest not being included in fishing-related compensation.
1997	Debate on fishing compensation is not yet resolved.

income since construction of the dam, including the 1,700 directly affected households.

Compensation Is a Moving Target in Implementing Resettlement

The relocation was extraordinarily easy. EGAT began civil works construction in May 1990 and completed the dam in April 1994. The reservoir was filled during the rainy season of 1994. Resettlement began in June 1990 and was completed by September 1994, with most of the people moving in the first half of 1994. Some households literally moved across the street. Most families moved less than a kilometer. Although the physical location was smooth, the process of achieving agreement on a package for compensation and income restoration package was much more complicated.

EGAT committed itself to improve the living standards of affected households, to provide a range of options, and to implement resettlement with the participation of the affected people. The issue was how to establish fair compensation.

EGAT's (base) resettlement policy of May 1990 stated that:

- Land would be compensated at the rate of $1,440 to $1,920 per hectare, the prevailing land price in 1990.
- Affected households could opt to have their houseplots raised (back-filled with earth) to 108.5 meters, or relocate and reconstruct their houses.
- Households opting for resettlement could either build their own houses and receive an additional grant of $5,400 each or accept a core house of two rooms in a resettlement area about 15 kilometers from the dam.

The base policy was modified several times. In 1991, owners of 73 farm plots rejected the resettlement terms, requesting a land survey by the district office. As a result, EGAT further enhanced the policy:

- Land compensation rates were quintupled, to seven to ten times the market value of unaffected land in the vicinity.
- Tenants (of both houses and farmland) were eligible for the same house and land compensation as legal owners.
- Households affected by dam-site construction would get full compensation, new houses, and 0.33–hectare houseplots.
- EGAT would provide all the civic infrastructure at the resettlement site.

The five-fold increase in the land compensation rate was largely due to extensive protests by resettlers and NGOs against the base policy rate. EGAT opted to pay the much higher rates to quell the increasing complaints against the construction of Pak Mun. This strategy succeeded in overcoming resistance. Unfortunately, the generous compensation rate led to severe inflation in land prices. By April 1993 land prices had escalated to 75 percent of the revised land compensation rate. Resettlers again protested for even more favorable compensation and resettlement packages. EGAT further amended the policy in May 1993:

- Households could opt for land purchased by EGAT in the vicinity of their original village (as opposed to the resettlement site, which no one chose).
- Households could opt for back-filling up to 0.5 hectare of farmland.
- All 234 households in the village closest to the dam site that might be affected by blasting (noise, flying debris) were offered compensation and relocation on the same terms as other affected households, or a $140 monthly subsidy until project completion.

Even in 1993, many resettlers were uncertain of what the consequences of the dam would be. They were unconvinced that the reservoir level would not rise higher than planned. In January 1994, families whose houses would be within 30 meters of the reservoir, or who would be excessively isolated by the reservoir, were also given the option of relocation with the full benefit package. In addition to the original 241 households, another 226 families inconvenienced by dam construction and 445 families above the flood level chose to relocate, mainly because of the generous cash compensation and the replacement house EGAT offered.

In April 1994, just before impoundment of the reservoir, a few hundred villagers and some NGOs protested against the project in Bangkok, claiming that the dam had already affected their fish catches, and demanded compensation for lost fishing income. As the baseline data on fishing income was inadequate, the government established a succession of mechanisms and committees to determine the effect of the dam on fishermen. Many households declined the first settlement offer, and the protests continued. In 1995, the government established the Committee on Assistance and Occupational Development for Fish Farmers, consisting of affected people, NGOs, EGAT, and the government. The Committee decided to compensate 2,932 households at a flat rate of $3,600, consisting of $1,200 in cash and $2,400 per household to fund cooperative activities on behalf of the fishermen. The reason for the cooperatives was to create a sustainable source of income. The cash component was to cover the transition period until the cooperatives could establish income-generating activities. As of mid-1996, some 3,000 additional households were seeking the compensation package for lost fishing income.

Actual Costs Considerably Exceed Planned Costs

Actual project costs were $233 million, compared with $178 million planned. (All costs in this chapter are converted at an exchange rate of 25 baht equals $1). Only 14 percent of the cost overrun was due to resettlement. Resettlement expenditures up to December 1993 totaled $19.7 million, a 67 percent cost overrun compared with the original budget provision of $11.8 million. Additional compensation has continued to be paid since then, primarily against claims of lost fishing income.

Compensation Is Generally Generous but Receives Mixed Responses

Households used compensation money for many things, but not principally for buying land. The largest single use of compensation money, about one-third, was savings. Many people put the money in the bank, and several older resettlers lived off the interest. Almost 24 percent was spent on house construction—mainly because some households opted to receive house compensation and build their own houses, rather than accept the EGAT two-room, core house, and then expand it to suit their needs. The other major use of compensation, 19 percent, was to share it with family members, especially children. Many resettlers helped their children to build houses, buy land, or get ahead in an occupation. Less than six percent of the total compensation received was spent on buying land.

Although resettlers are naturally inclined to say that what they have received so far is inadequate, to make the case for additional benefits, evidence is overwhelming that compensation rates for houses and land were generous and that this is recognized by the resettlers, if only indirectly. The fact that compensation was so generous has generated discontent among noncompensated (unaffected) people. This is one of the best indicators that compensation was more than adequate and is confirmed by survey data showing that unaffected people would have liked to have been resettled themselves if they could have received compensation.

The focus of resettler displeasure was on the compensation for lost fishing income. The fishing compensation issue was not handled well. All those compensated received the same compensation package regardless of whether they fished part time for home consumption or earned most of their living from fishing. Those who were full-time fishermen and primarily dependent on fishing for income probably did not receive adequate compensation.

The other major source of frustration was all the minor inconveniences of being relocated that were not directly compensated for. For example, as land became scarcer, previously unfenced land that could be grazed was no longer available. Many people have chosen to sell off their herds. Because of reduced forest area, people no longer collect bamboo, mushrooms, and other materials in any significant quantity. Riverbank vegetable gardens are far scarcer now. Neither forests nor riverbank gardens were compensated because, by law, neither can be privately owned. Transportation times and costs have increased where tributaries are now swollen much of the year. Wells for drinking water have to be sunk deeper at greater cost. The compensation committee established to handle the grievances has not resolved many of the problems of individual households. However, the compensation rates are believed to have more than made up for these inconveniences, for those who received compensation.

With Income Restoration, Incomes Are Maintained and the Quality of Life Is Improved

The primary principle of the resettlement strategy was to offer as many options as necessary to ensure that the fewest people suffered hardships because of the project. The original plan provided each family with an irrigated farmplot of at least 1.6 hectares in the proposed resettlement area. Once it became evident that no one would choose this option, EGAT abandoned further development of the site and people were compensated and were free to spend the compensation money as they saw fit. In that sense, there was no organized income restoration strategy.

Most of the resettler households' farmland was upland and therefore not affected, although a minor amount of good rice-growing lowlands was flooded. More than two-thirds of the 200 inundated households lost no farmland, and only 12 lost three hectares or more. Because they purchased just enough replacement land, now each of these households have almost as much land, 3.5 hectares, as it had before dam construction. Therefore, the income restoration strategy was

TABLE 4.2
Annual Household Incomes

Sources of Income ($ Per Household in the Previous 12 Months)[a]	Rural Hhds. 1983	House-Losers 1994	House-Losers 1996	Land-Losers 1996	Unaffected Hhds. 1996
Number of households	253	219	200	50	50
Crops, trees, vegetables	765	120	150	210	115
Livestock	295	225	290	450	235
Fish, shrimp	105	605	350	530	270
Subtotal farm income	1,165	950	790	1,190	620
Salaries		385	395	95	135
Other wages	400	765	700	215	425
Building contracts		35	130	90	15
Brokering, interest		55	125	440	145
Handicrafts	10	55	95	45	5
Trading	65	420	260	220	815
Income from migration		120	180	115	240
Other nonfarm income	320	45	125	210	30
Subtotal nonfarm income	795	1,880	2,010	1,430	1,810
Total income	1,960	2,830	2,800	2,620	2,430

[a] All income figures are converted at the 1997 exchange rate of 25 baht = 1 dollar and are adjusted for 45 percent inflation from 1983–94 and 13 percent inflation from 1994–96.

NOTE: Some house-loser households also lost land, and some land-loser households lost houses, but the three groups are categorized by their principal form of loss (and compensation). Households in all three 1996 groups lost income from fishing. Other nonfarm income includes land, animal, and tool rental; collection of forest products; and gambling. Income categories in 1983 are not identical to 1994 and 1996 categories.

SOURCES: Data for 1983 are from *Environmental and Ecological Investigation of Pak Mun Project*, TEAM Consulting Engineers and Mahidol University, 1984. Data for 1994 and 1996 are from Khon Kaen University's two surveys.

primarily not based on land use. Many affected people took the opportunity to further shift income to nonfarm sources, but this process was well under way before the dam.

Surveys in 1994 (just after resettlement) and 1996 show that average household incomes have increased in current terms and held almost steady in constant terms, but that varies widely between households. Sources of income have shifted (see table 4.2). Before resettlement (despite the land-based nature of EGAT's first resettlement plan), incomes were already largely not based on land use. Resettlement further encouraged, supported, and accelerated the move to nonfarm income. In many cases people could see that returns to their labor were much greater in the secondary and tertiary sectors than in agriculture, given the generally low quality of soil and poor yields in this part of Thailand. A significant amount of the growth in nonfarm income came from migration. Both permanent migration (more than six months per year) and temporary migration (less than six months) significantly increased from 1994 to 1996.

TABLE 4.3
Household Assets

Household Assets (Percentage of Households Owning Asset)	Rural Hhds. 1983	House-Losers 1991	House-Losers 1994	House-Losers 1996	Land-Losers 1991	Land-Losers 1996	Unaffected Hhds. 1991	Unaffected Hhds. 1996
Number of households	253	200	219	200	50	50	50	50
Motorcycle	7	30	63	70	28	72	22	24
Bicycle	50	63	66	64	62	66	44	54
Color television		22	45	66	12	86	22	56
Black & white TV	15	47	44	33	56	20	40	46
Stereo		20	42	42	22	54	22	42
Radio	89	71	60	62	64	40	56	48
Sewing machine	12	16	14	18	20	32	6	12
Electric fan	5	60	84	85	46	94	46	92
Electric iron	6	27	32	44	18	46	18	36
Electric pan		18	28	34	14	36	14	26
Electric rice cooker		31	46	57	28	70	22	48
Refrigerator		20	34	52	18	76	18	38
Gas stove		3	7	12	0	24	8	10

SOURCES: Data fro 1983 are from Environmental and Ecological Investigation of Pak *Mun Project*, TEAM Consulting Engineers and Mahidol University, 1984. Data for 1991, 1994, and 1996 are from Khon Kaen University's two surveys.

Fish catch and income decreased almost 50 percent over the two year period and may have already been declining before 1994. This is significant, as fish income accounted for almost two-thirds of farm income in 1994, and still counted for almost one-half of farm income in 1996. Most fishermen claim that the dam has inhibited fish migration, scoured the riverbed, reduced the river's oxygen content, and interfered with fish spawning. Fishing is undoubtedly more difficult than before the dam, especially given the simple equipment and methods that many of the fishermen use. While fishing income has decreased significantly, shrimping—an income source not even envisioned before dam construction—has replaced much of that.

Incomes have increased primarily because of spontaneous actions by resettlers rather than because of organized options designed by the government. The rapid growth of the Thai economy has made this possible. Resettler unemployment declined from ten percent in 1994 to nine percent in 1996. (No one mentioned any difficulty in finding a job). Although two-thirds of the resettlers described their principal occupation as farming, it accounted for only four percent of their total income. The dam and reservoir had little effect on farming income and a questionable effect on fishing, and alternative sources of income made up most of the losses. In fact, the compensation made more changes possible than the lost income caused.

Besides income, other aspects of quality of life improved as well. Housing was the most important single asset among resettlers. The quality of resettler housing definitely improved. Most resettlers had one-story, wood houses with an earthen, open ground floor before the dam. Now the predominant category is two-story, wood and cement houses, with cement-enclosed ground floors.

Almost every type of household asset is dramatically increasing in number among the resettlers (see table 4.3). The increase has been significant, even allowing for the general increased welfare of the Thai people. People now have color TVs, stereos, video players, and motorcycles. The land-losers on average are the best off, the house-losers are slightly behind them, and the unaffected households are a bit farther behind. Farm assets have likewise increased. They would probably be even higher had not so many households shifted their economic activities away from farming.

EGAT improved many social services. Before dam construction, people relied on a variety of sources for their water supply. EGAT provided piped water systems to all resettler houses. Receiving a tap-water supply was one of the most important reasons for resettler satisfaction. EGAT also provided electrical connections to all the resettler houses that did not have electricity (except for a handful of houses rebuilt far from any village), greatly improved the road system, built new health facilities in many of the villages, constructed or rehabilitated schools, and provided much other infrastructure. The government has provided many other services as well, including a $600,000 fishery development program, vocational training in eight occupational specialties, and a health impact mitigation program.

Resettlers Complain Despite Improvements

Despite the generous compensation for houses and land, as well as many other social infrastructure and service benefits, many people claim to be worse off. There is such a culture of complaint to win sympathy for greater compensation claims that it is difficult to get affected people to be objective about their resettlement experience. People claim to dislike the development or modernization process, of which the dam looms large in their minds, but that is only one small part of the change sweeping rural northeastern Thailand.

Resettler opinion about the project is sharply divided. Most are at least somewhat satisfied. The unaffected people that lost fishing income only, and that did not receive compensation for lost houses or land, have much more negative attitudes. This group appears to have suffered a decrease in income, at least among many of its members. Resettlers are most unhappy about the decreased fish catch, and that is overwhelmingly (74 percent) the most frequent complaint. They also are dissatisfied with the loss of vegetables growing along the riverbanks, especially during the dry season, and the loss of access to forest products. The many inconveniences to daily life contribute to their dissatisfaction.

Electricity Generating Authority of Thailand Could Afford Excellent Resettlement Performance

EGAT's resettlement performance was excellent, primarily in response to the tremendous amount of public criticism over the Pak Mun project, and out of all proportion to its defects. While EGAT did get off to a poor start, it recovered well and has systematically addressed practically every complaint concerning resettlement. It could be argued that EGAT's very willingness to be responsive to criticism exacerbated compensation complaints. Even three years after the project, EGAT, the NGOs, and the resettlers have an extraordinary level of personal familiarity, interaction, and generally good personal relations with each other.

Planning was deficient in several regards, but not fatally flawed. The original design would have created a reservoir that would have backed up to the regional capital of Ubon Ratchathani. It would have converted the entire lower reaches of the river into a lake. EGAT modified the design until it became a run-of-the-river dam with storage limited mainly to the normal high-water level during the rainy season. This is a "best practice" example of minimizing resettlement, although at significant cost to the power benefits of the project, which were reduced by 33 percent. Land compensation rates matched the prevailing market price, but land inflation is practically unavoidable and should have been anticipated. By offering the existing market price, EGAT had to revise rates later, and thus initiated the pattern of NGOs' and resettlers' protesting existing rates and eventually agreeing to much higher rates.

The two committees established by the government to manage resettlement set high standards, with which EGAT fully complied. This created a situation in which the committee could dictate to EGAT how to spend EGAT money; thus the committee could make decisions with little accountability for the costs incurred. Fortunately, EGAT is a profitable company. Pak Mun was a relatively inexpensive project for EGAT, and the dam affected relatively few people, so the resettlement costs could be readily absorbed. EGAT could afford to be generous at Pak Mun, and it was.

Resettlers Provide Major Inputs, but Not Soon Enough

EGAT got off to a bad start. Communication, resettler participation, and relations with the resettlers were poor at first. People could not make rational decisions in the face of so much uncertainty. For example, the choice of the initial resettlement site, which apparently was made without consulting the resettlers, wasted considerable time and money. Resettlers rarely want to move farther than the minimal distance possible, and since the inundation impacts were minor, resettlers saw no need to move to a consolidated site more than five kilometers from the river. After this initial difficult and confrontational period, lasting until 1993, EGAT was responsive to resettlers' demands to modify resettlement options. However, by putting the resettlers on the defensive at the outset, EGAT later had to expend extra effort and money to regain their goodwill and trust.

When it became clear that the proposed resettlement site was objectionable to resettlers, EGAT readily agreed to other options they proposed. EGAT increased land compensation rates fivefold. Resettlers' suggestions led to a variety of other modifications. The committees for compensating lost fishing incomes included resettlers. EGAT spent $1 million on community relations and public information programs, holding hundreds of meetings.

Settler Dissatisfaction Feeds Nongovernmental Organization Agenda

Project relations with NGOs were more difficult. The NGOs accused EGAT of not giving them information and consistently refused to enter into a dialogue. Pak Mun was strongly opposed by the Thai NGO, Project for Ecological Recovery, which is opposed to the construction of all dams. Several hundred Thai and international NGOs joined the protests against the dam under that organization's coalition leadership. More than half the resettlers joined the NGO protests, mainly to get improved resettlement packages, not to stop dam construction. As EGAT continued to improve the package and develop better relations with the resettlers, support for the NGOs diminished. Most resettlers realize they have benefited from the NGO protests on their behalf but have come to terms with EGAT on most issues. The primary resettlement issue that remains contentious is compensation for lost fishing income. The NGOs now criticize Pak Mun primarily for environmental effects, not resettlement issues.

Conclusions

Minimizing resettlement greatly reduced potential negative publicity and financial exposure. Although this did not prevent the intense antidam protest movement, the dam redesign was worthwhile. The original design, with 16 times as many inundated families, would have been exponentially more expensive to implement to the same standards.

EGAT should have had better consultation with resettlers to determine what income restoration strategies they would be likely to choose. However, resettlers can always change their minds as conditions change. To some extent, Pak Mun was overtaken by events. By the time the dam was built, the resettlers no longer depended primarily on farm-based incomes. Thailand's booming economy offered many more attractive options than the low returns from farming. By the time the resettlers had to move in 1994, few of them cared to buy replacement land.

The lack of an updated baseline survey came back to haunt EGAT. Land compensation became the central contentious issue, but the number of land-losing households was not known until September 1991, more than a year into project work. In 1994, when the issue of compensation for lost fishing income arose, once again the lack of baseline data made analyzing and challenging resettler claims difficult. EGAT has paid a high price for what appeared to be a relatively minor oversight at the time.

Compensation was so generous that it led to jealousy and fraudulent claims. The compensation itself led to much of the successful income restoration, even though that was not the plan. People have been able to diversify their livelihoods precisely because their neighbors now have money to spend on those services and products.

Fishing compensation, the main remaining contentious issue, may ultimately work out for the best. The Department of Fisheries is rapidly developing the reservoir fishery and learning more about which species work best. It has been creative, for example, by introducing shrimp. Flexible adaptation is the key to success. With enough commitment, most obstacles can be overcome.

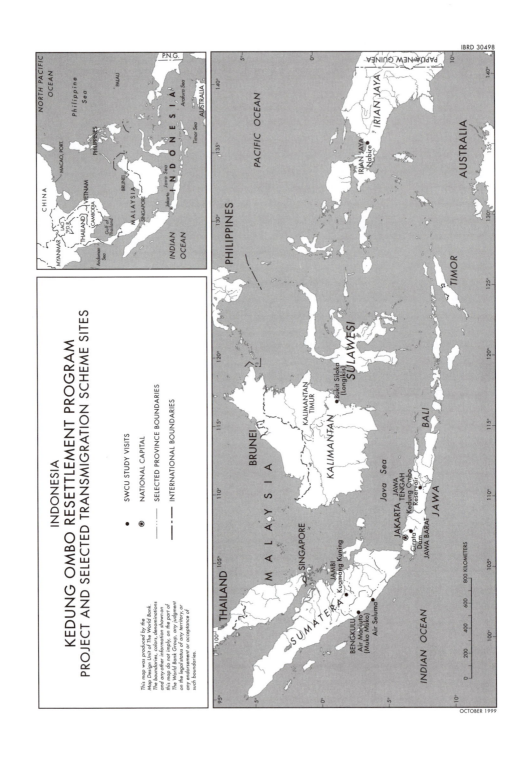

INDONESIA
KEDUNG OMBO RESETTLEMENT PROGRAM
PROJECT AND SELECTED TRANSMIGRATION SCHEME SITES

● SWCU STUDY VISITS

⊕ NATIONAL CAPITAL

–––– SELECTED PROVINCE BOUNDARIES

––––– INTERNATIONAL BOUNDARIES

This map was produced by the
Map Design Unit of The World Bank.
The boundaries, colors, denominations
and any other information shown on
this map do not imply, on the part of
The World Bank Group, any judgment
on the legal status of any territory, or
any endorsement or acceptance of
such boundaries.

IBRD 30498

OCTOBER 1999

5

Poor Planning and Settler Resistance in Indonesia

The Kedung Ombo experience is important as an extreme example of the conflict that can result when poor planning for resettlement by the authorities combines with almost total absence of input from those to be resettled. The Indonesian government has pursued a program of "transmigration" for many years, to take pressure off the very densely populated island of Java by moving families to new settlements in the sparsely populated outer islands (map IBRD 30498). The government expected that most displacees from the Kedung Ombo dam project in Central Java would join the transmigration program, and an early survey of families to be affected by the dam supported this expectation.

However, when the time came, most families refused to move for various reasons:

- Land compensation was inadequate for resettlers to purchase equivalent holdings in Java.
- The government refused to consider higher compensation.
- No plans had been made to assist displacees learn new cropping technologies or off-farm skills to succeed in new, less fertile settlements in Java.

Furthermore, some of these people were political opponents of the Suharto regime, already distrustful of government. Under pressure to move people out of the reservoir area, authorities used coercive measures.

The confrontation between government and displacees received international publicity and ultimately resulted in a relaxation on restrictions as to where displacees could move, a technical assistance effort for resettlers that was merely a Band-Aid and was not very successful, and new policies to avoid such problems in future projects. Despite the conflicts, most of the resettlers believe they are better off now than they were before the move (although there are notable exceptions in the transmigration areas), even without government help in income

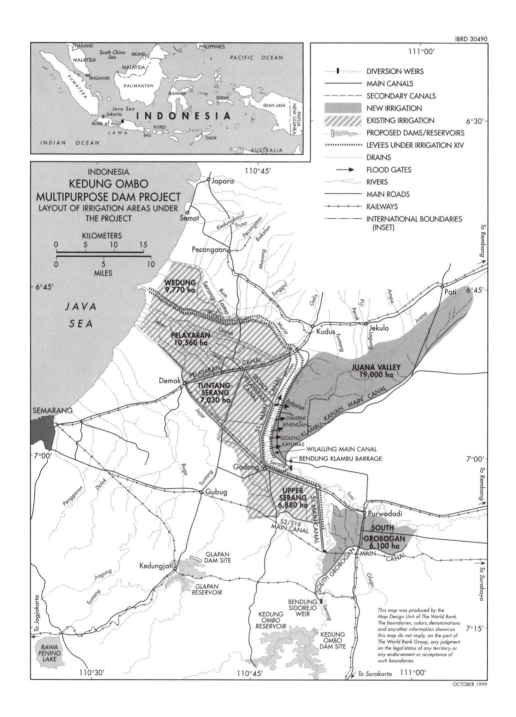

IBRD 30490

THAILAND
South China Sea
MALAYSIA
SINGAPORE
SUMATERA
INDIAN OCEAN
Jakarta
Java Sea
JAWA
Area of map
Bali
FLORES
TIMOR
JAVA
BRUNEI
PHILIPPINES
PACIFIC OCEAN
KALIMANTAN
SULAWESI
SERAM
IRIAN JAYA
PAPUA NEW GUINEA
INDONESIA
AUSTRALIA

DIVERSION WEIRS
MAIN CANALS
SECONDARY CANALS
NEW IRRIGATION
EXISTING IRRIGATION
PROPOSED DAMS/RESERVOIRS
LEVEES UNDER IRRIGATION XIV
DRAINS
FLOOD GATES
RIVERS
MAIN ROADS
RAILWAYS
INTERNATIONAL BOUNDARIES (INSET)

111°00'
6°30'

INDONESIA
KEDUNG OMBO
MULTIPURPOSE DAM PROJECT
LAYOUT OF IRRIGATION AREAS UNDER
THE PROJECT

KILOMETERS
0   5   10   15
0   5   10
MILES

JAVA SEA

Japara
Semat
Kedungbajul
Truso
Pecangaan
Bokalan
Pecangaan
Mayong
Tungaul
Gelis
Muria
Piji
Perak
Ampo
To Rembang

WEDUNG
9,770 ha
Serang Lama
Bum
Wulan
Cajol
Jago
Sedad
PELAYARAN
10,560 ha
PELAYARAN CANAL
Demak
TUNTANG-SERANG
7,030 ha
Jojor
Jajar
Kudus
Tuntang
Jekulo
Laguno
Juana
Pati
6°45'

SEMARANG
7°00'

PELAYARAN CANAL
SEDAD CANAL
S1 MAIN CANAL
MURIA CANAL
JUANA VALLEY
19,000 ha
Bobolan
DAMPAK
JENENGAN
GOLENG
KAYUMAS
KLAMBU
KANAN MAIN CANAL
WILALUNG MAIN CANAL
BENDUNG KLAMBU BARRAGE
Serang

Godong
Bugo
Tuntang
Dolok
Penggaron
Gubug

UPPER SERANG
6,880 ha
S1 MAIN CANAL
S2/S16 MAIN CANAL
SOUTH GROBOGAN MAIN CANAL
Lusi
Purwodadi
SOUTH GROBOGAN
6,100 ha
Glagu
To Rembang
To Surabaya

7°00'

GLAPAN DAM SITE
GLAPAN RESERVOIR
Kedungjati
Jragang
Tuntang

BENDUNG SIDOREJO WEIR
Serang
KEDUNG OMBO RESERVOIR
KEDUNG OMBO DAM SITE

This map was produced by the
Map Design Unit of The World Bank.
The boundaries, colors, denominations
and any other information shown on
this map do not imply, on the part of
The World Bank Group, any judgment
on the legal status of any territory, or
any endorsement or acceptance of
such boundaries.

7°15'

To Jogjakarta
RAWA PENING LAKE
110°30'
110°45'
To Surakarta
111°00'

OCTOBER 1999

TABLE 5.1
Project Chronology

Date	Event
1981	Initial survey indicates 5,400 households need to be moved, of which at least 4,000 prefer transmigration off Java.
1983–84	Small groups leave for transmigration sites in Irian Jaya, Sumatra and Jambi
1985	Dam construction begins with World Bank loan.
1986-88	Large out-migration takes place, mainly self-settlers who take compensation but relocate themselves.
1987	Jakarta-based NGO advocacy groups allege the government is using coercive tactics to force relocation among residents unwilling to move; international NGOs and media focus attention.
1998, January	Dam construction completed, gates are closed to begin filling reservoir.
1988, April	Project monitoring contractor confirms local people's reluctance to move: despite government estimates that 3,000 families had transmigrated, the actual figure was only 400.
1987-88	Though unwilling to increase compensation, government recognizes families will not transmigrate. Three nearby settlements are prepared and resettlement begins. Government also eases pressure on villagers who stay in the greenbelt zone above the dam, though it remains illegal.
1989	Government and World Bank begin Kedung Ombo Resettlement & Reservoir Development Program (RRPP) to help non-transmigrant resettlers adjust to new lands and cropping methods.
1990, April	Reservoir is completely filled.
1993	Dam project and RRDP end.
1993	Government officially agrees settlers can stay on the greenbelt.
1993	Government issues two Presidential Decrees guaranteeing resident participation in resettlement process and improving compensation guidelines.
1993	Supreme Court awards compensation for lost land to 34 plaintiffs in the greenbelt, substantially above levels previously demanded.
1994	Supreme Court cancels its previous ruling and advises plaintiffs to start again, exposing Indonesian government to further criticism.

recovery. Their success is a reflection of the tremendous growth of the Indonesian economy (see table 5.1).

With Dense Population, Displacees Should Want to Transmigrate

About 50 kilometers southeast of Semarang, the provincial capital on the north coast of Central Java, the Kedung Ombo dam intersects a river system that once annually restored the fertility of the river valleys and part of the floodplains (see map IBRD 30490). The reservoir inundated most of this intensively farmed land. The reservoir extends to the south and west to a maximum length of 15 kilometers. The reservoir area is part of a hilly upland framed by several mountain ranges, with deeply weathered rock unsuitable for high-productivity agriculture.

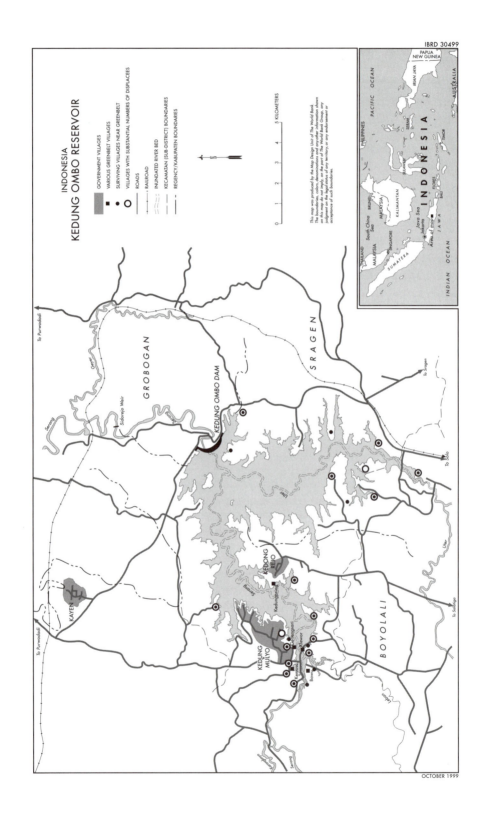

IBRD 30499

INDONESIA
KEDUNG OMBO RESERVOIR

GOVERNMENT VILLAGES
VARIOUS GREENBELT VILLAGES
SURVIVING VILLAGES NEAR GREENBELT
VILLAGES WITH SUBSTANTIAL NUMBERS OF DISPLACEES
ROADS
RAILROAD
INUNDATED RIVER BED
KECAMATAN (SUB-DISTRICT) BOUNDARIES
REGENCY/KABUPATEN BOUNDARIES

0   1   2   3   4   5 KILOMETERS

This map was produced by the Map Design Unit of The World Bank.
The boundaries, colors, denominations and any other information shown
on this map do not imply, on the part of The World Bank Group, any
judgment on the legal status of any territory, or any endorsement or
acceptance of such boundaries.

OCTOBER 1999

The reservoir occupied parts of three regencies (map IBRD 30499). Most of the occupied land, most of the people threatened by displacement, and all of the extensive southwestern floodplain belonged to Kemusu district of Boyolali.[1] Coincidentally, Kemusu was an important center of repressed resistance by radical groups driven underground by the military action of 1965.[2]

Kemusu was the center of the controversy that arose over compensation rates for displacees, suitable substitute sites, and the insistence to stay put and cultivate the greenbelt as well as the fertile old floodplain as it reemerged every year when water was released for irrigation (the drawdown area). This controversy shaped the resettlement experience of Kedung Ombo. The Kedung Ombo hills are among the least attractive parts of the province for subsistence agriculture. Eventually, 4,800 families moved out of the reservoir. Another 600 families stayed in—or shifted up to but not beyond—the greenbelt zone that was meant to be cleared of human habitation (map IBRD 30500).

There were four categories of resettlers. The largest category consists of self-settled households that moved up into or next to the traditional villages surrounding the lake. Most had accepted a compensation package that covered their previous land holdings and houses. The second category consists of the households that entered one of three new villages that the government built for the displacees next to (Kedungmulyo and Kedungrejo) or a short distance from (Kayen) the lake. All these resettlers had to accept a compensation package for at least one of their fields before entering the new villages. These resettlers had to adjust to poorer soils on higher ground unless they retained access to part of the greenbelt or drawdown areas (map IBRD 30500).

A third category consists of the households that remained living in or just below the greenbelt, in the prohibited zones immediately above the reservoir's full supply level. The zone of lakeside land between the water line, at 90.5 meters, and 92.5 meters, was reserved to accommodate unusual floods, although it was expected to remain dry in most years. The next higher prohibited zone between 92.5 meters and 95.0 meters was the greenbelt, which was to remain forever dry but protected against human habitation, erosion, and any other uses that threatened the integrity of the reservoir. Households that refused to abandon the reservoir are concentrated in the greenbelt. Some live in the flood zone. No one lives in the drawdown zone, although much of it is extensively farmed when it is accessible. The best estimates are that two-thirds of the original greenbelt farmers (that is, not the new households) have never accepted compensation, and that two-thirds of all households that never accepted compensation are in the greenbelt.

The fourth category consists of the households, and parts of households that joined the official transmigration program and were transported to resettlement schemes on the outer islands.

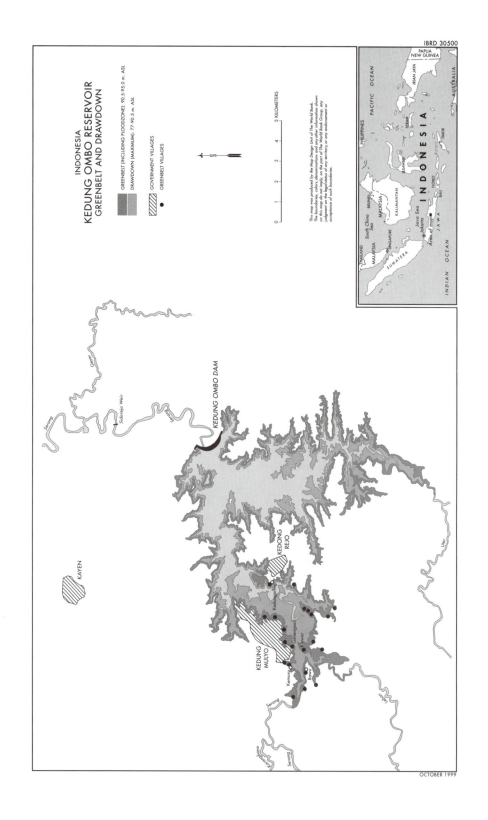

INDONESIA

KEDUNG OMBO RESERVOIR
GREENBELT AND DRAWDOWN

GREENBELT (INCLUDING FLOODZONE): 90.5-95.0 m. ASL

DRAWDOWN (MAXIMUM): 77-90.5 m. ASL

GOVERNMENT VILLAGES

● GREENBELT VILLAGES

0   1   2   3   4   5 KILOMETERS

This map was produced by the Map Design Unit of The World Bank.
The boundaries, colors, denominations and any other information shown
on this map do not imply, on the part of The World Bank Group, any
judgment on the legal status of any territory, or any endorsement or
acceptance of such boundaries.

IBRD 30500

OCTOBER 1999

A 1993 survey estimated the number of resettler families in each category:

Self-settled	2,800
In government-built villages	700
In the greenbelt	600
Transmigrant	1,300

This excludes households formed subsequent to the initial estimates. The government-village and greenbelt figures should each be increased by about 200 to reflect those new households.

The Kedung Ombo resettlement program grossly misjudged the sizes of these categories of displacees. A 1981 assessment indicated that some 5,300 families would have to be relocated, estimating that 75 to 80 percent of the families were inclined to opt for transmigration. In fact, only 1,300 became transmigrants. This inaccurate estimate is probably the most important factor explaining the debacle that was to occur. It relieved planners and implementers of the task of preparing alternative resettlement and income-generation operations. It took attention away from the inadequacy of the compensation formulas for expropriating land from nontransmigrants.

There has been debate over the reason so many displaced families chose to remain in the locality after originally stating an intention to transmigrate. Some people may have found it too difficult to envision the enormous change such a shift would entail. Some may have learned that the transmigration sites were unprepared.

One problem with the ex post estimates of transmigration was that there were no means to count the number of Kedung Ombo displacees among the streams of transmigrants. The Boyolali and Sragen regencies both aimed to attend to the displacees. However, their quotas and records were based on regency, not project, rolls, and they did not try to ascertain the legitimacy of a volunteer's claim that he was a displacee from the reservoir. These records were the basis for the government's reports in the critical period 1985–87 that resettlement was proceeding as expected.

The projections of transmigrants turned out to be overoptimistic because no one was responsible for creating attractive conditions at the sites to induce the flow. The ex post estimates of self-directed displacees and legitimate transmigrants are shaky because no one was responsible for counting either group. By contrast, the numbers of households in the three government villages and the greenbelt are known exactly; in fact, the occupation of the greenbelt has been closely observed. Nevertheless, the two largest categories are the self-settlers and transmigrants with about 75 percent of the total, and these are the figures that are inexact.

The World Bank's loan became effective in November 1985 following award of the contracts for construction and supervision of the dam. The main implementing agency was the Jratunseluna River Basin Development Project Office, a dependency of the Directorate General for Water Resources Development headquartered in Semarang. Engineering works on the dam, weirs, and irrigation infrastructure were well implemented and completed on schedule. The gates were closed to begin filling the reservoir on January 14, 1988.

Initially the Project Office left resettlement activities mostly to the Ministry of Home Affairs and the provincial government, and special committees were set up at provincial and regency levels to supervise and coordinate this work. The provincial administration was responsible for determining general levels of compensation for each category of land and other assets, village-level government officials followed these guidelines in determining awards to individual families, and the regency administration was responsible for ensuring that all eligible families were paid. The project did not provide any funds for developing infrastructure and other facilities for resettlers remaining in the area. Nor did it provide for transmigration. However, transmigration costs were well known, and the government was committed to providing cash payments to the Ministry of Transmigration for Kedung Ombo families, as it did for all others.

Small groups of oustees from the reservoir began to leave for transmigration sites in Sumatra and Irian Jaya in 1983. Small groups from Sragen arrived in Jambi in November 1984. However, mass movement under transmigration did not start until 1988, when the Muko Muko irrigation scheme in Bengkulu Province, Sumatra, was ready to accept Kedung Ombo applicants. Families opting for self-settlement were moving throughout this period, before 1986 from Sragen[3] and after 1986 from Kemusu. The institution monitoring resettlement delivered its first report in April 1988. It was this report that alerted the government that previous estimates of the numbers of families that had already left the reservoir were grossly exaggerated. While the government had estimated that about 3,000 families had departed from Boyolali and Sragen under the transmigration program alone, the monitoring contractor found that fewer than 400 families genuinely threatened by the reservoir had actually left.

This news confirmed alarming reports by NGOs that the resettlement component was stuck at the starting gate. The first substantial report chronicled incidents reported by villagers of the government's rough handling of the families resisting the move, a report provided informally to the Bank in September 1987 by the Legal Aid Institute.[4] The incidents are alleged to have included physical violence, but the worst injuries were psychological and social. Government and military officials in some cases allegedly stamped or threatened to stamp the identity cards of recalcitrant heads of families with marks indicating a record as a political prisoner or membership with an outlawed organization. These marks would have been enough to stigmatize that person and prevent access to certain jobs and other benefits. Most families feared that the consequences would be more severe, carrying over to all jobs and other family members and descendants. The regency government encouraged these fears. The threat of such markings was enough to convince many families to accept compensation and leave.

The Project Office maintained the momentum of its dam-building program. It closed the gates in January 1988. There were still about 1,500 families below the

95-meter line. By May, the number was down to 790; by January 1989, to 740. Six traditional Kemusu villages dominated that list.

The collision between government officials intent on emptying the reservoir and a politically charged populace that refused to move on government's terms was followed closely by the Indonesian press and amply described in other documents. The most persuasive is a nearly unemotional[5] presentation of the historical record issued in July 1995 by an international NGO, the Lawyers Committee for Human Rights, and its Indonesian collaborator, the Institute for Policy Research and Advocacy (ELSAM): *In the Name of Development: Human Rights and the World Bank in Indonesia.* The worst incidents at Kedung Ombo—chronicled by LBH and retold by ELSAM—would be enough for many readers to agree that no benefits below the dam could justify this behavior above it.

The ELSAM report describes the later events that were to expose the government to even more criticism. In 1993, Indonesia's Supreme Court rejected a lower court ruling and awarded compensation for lost land to 34 plaintiffs from the village of Kedungpring in the greenbelt, the new site of one out of six villages, and determined to resist at any price. The court's award was substantially above levels previously demanded, including in the petition itself. One year later the same high court, with a different chief justice, canceled the previous ruling and advised the Kedungpring group to start again. The decision probably finishes the legal action on compensation and closes that part of the story of the Kemusu rebellion.

Parallel to these ugly events, the government began in mid-1987 to seek other resettlement sites in Central Java. It recognized that most households would now refuse transmigration and that land compensation rates were too low to allow all households to buy substitute land close to the reservoir. After a protracted search, three public forest reserves were prepared for settlement, with roads, water, electricity, public buildings, and houses of worship. With a few exceptions, the resettlers were obliged to build their own homes. The first resettlers moved to Kayen in 1988, and to Kedungrejo and Kedungmulyo the next year (map IBRD 30500). Kedungmulyo, north of the village of Kemusu, was the only one of these sites to have access to both greenbelt and drawdown land and reasonably good rainfed soils.

The reservoir filled gradually, finally topping off at 90 meters in April 1990. The slow rise in the lake was in response to low rainfall levels in the catchment and requirements for water downstream. The authorities never repressed the lake level for the purpose of ensuring a more orderly evacuation of the displacees. The government was convinced that regardless of the battle over compensation, the households under threat of inundation had the time they needed to move up and ahead of the approaching water.

This assumption proved correct. Resisting families moved with the water, some at the last moment. Most of those that retreated to the greenbelt subsequently improved their temporary homes and joined the previous occupiers of the greenbelt in holding out for permanent residency. Others kept going. It appears that the number of families living in the greenbelt reached its low point of about 530 in late 1989—exactly ten percent of the number of families that had been projected to move. Most of the men had left to work in cities, leaving family members behind.

A little over a year after the gates were closed, and before the water reached the full supply level of 90.5 meters, government began to relax its pressure on greenbelt families to keep moving. Then families began moving back to the greenbelt. By 1993, there were approximately 600 families living in the greenbelt, growing to 915 families by 1997. Compensation had been overtaken by an equally compelling demand—to keep the greenbelt and drawdown under crops."

As pressure on the residents diminished, many of them in turn shifted their aim from higher compensation—in order to leave—to no compensation—in order to stay. At stake were about 9,000 hectares, perhaps half of it prime cultivable land, and perhaps three-quarters of that in the drawdown (in good years). In 1993, 3,000 farmers controlled 3,900 parcels of land in the greenbelt, and an overlapping set of another 3,000 farmers controlled 4,500 parcels in the (maximum) drawdown.[6]

By 1993 government made it official—the farmers would be allowed to stay in the greenbelt, but they could not build new permanent structures and would not be provided with teachers and other public services. Since then new building has proceeded without objection and the greenbelt is filling up. There were 815 households in Kemusu in 1997 (and approximately 100 more scattered along the slopes in Sragen). Ex-titles to the parcels (the government "owns" them all now) are a tradable commodity, and some families use them like pieces in a chess game. They may accept compensation for one or two, to gain rights to Kedungmulyo, but keep others for a family member's home and for farming.

Income Recovery Intervention Is Too Late and Too Brief

The original design assumed that most of the resettlers would move to transmigration sites. There, cleared land, physical infrastructure, and technical assistance were provided in support of one or another income-generating scheme. Muko Muko on Sumatra and Nabire on Irian Jaya were designed as irrigation schemes, Bukit Saloka in East Kalimantan was designed for smallholder oil palm plantations, and Kuamang Kuning on Sumatra was planned for a consortium of rainfed food and cash crops. However, no plans were made to support resettlers who opted to move themselves within Central Java. The assumption was they would be serviced, if they needed support, by the province's line technical departments.

By 1989 that omission was no longer defensible. The World Bank and the government agreed to rebuild the resettlement program. The new program, titled the Kedung Ombo Resettlement and Reservoir Development Program (RRDP), was approved in September 1989. The Bank reallocated $7 million of loan funds to support the program.

RRDP operated through a series of contracts with four local universities and an NGO to provide research, extension, and other services. These started in 1991 and included:

- Fishery studies and pilot programs for capture and cage fishing
- Research and extension on appropriate technologies for exploiting the drawdown zone, on one hand, and the dry upland areas, on the other hand
- Research and extension on management of the greenbelt zone to protect the reservoir while maximizing economic use by resettlers consistent with protection.

Follow-up contracts were signed to continue monitoring the relocation and assess the socioeconomic impacts on resettlers. Subsequently, contracts were also signed to:

- Prepare an environmental management and monitoring plan
- Investigate sociolegal aspects of occupation of the drawdown and greenbelt zones
- Provide extension support for home industry and commercial activity in the three government villages.

RRDP was a massive program through the end of 1993, when the Bank's involvement was completed. Virtually none of the programs survived the Bank's exit. Some of the university activity designs were later described as overly academic. One example was the crop models for upland cropping, which called for rates of application of manure beyond the typical family's means and even beyond supplies in local markets. In addition, local government ownership of the successful project activities never developed. The commitment of the provincial line agencies was lukewarm throughout 1989–93. When the project ended in 1993, the agencies terminated most of the services aimed exclusively at the reservoir area.

Transmigration Has Mixed Results, with Resettlement Sites Scattered

About 1,250 families moved to 17 transmigration sites on Sumatra, Kalimantan, and Irian Jaya. The four largest clusters are described below.

Muko Muko, Bengkulu Province, Sumatra. This was a paddy irrigation scheme for four subschemes supplied by a weir feeding the left bank of the Air Manjuto River. Only about 310 genuinely displaced families moved in, which still makes it the largest Kedung Ombo reservoir resettlement colony. All settlers got a 0.25-hectare houselot, a 0.75-hectare plot cleared and irrigated, and another one-hectare lot with irrigation structures but not otherwise cleared. An inexplicable error was made in site planning, because half of the forest area cleared and supplied with irrigation on the left bank was underlain by a medium to thick strata of peat.

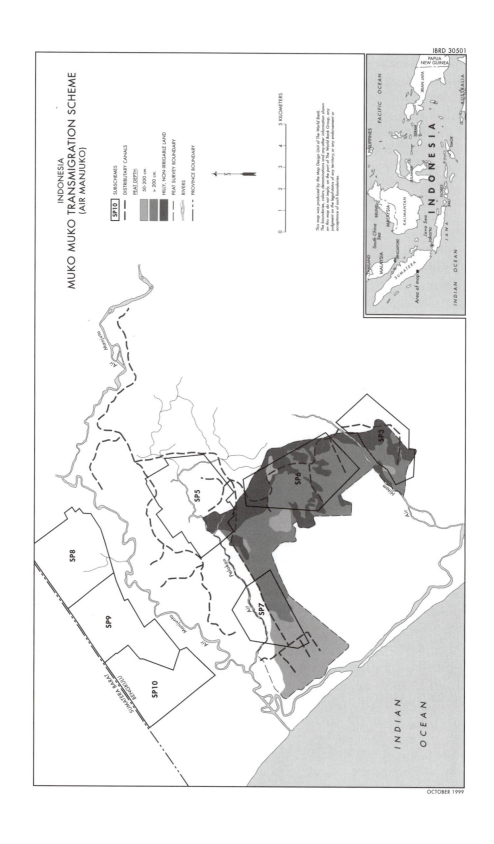

INDONESIA
MUKO MUKO TRANSMIGRATION SCHEME
(AIR MANJUKO)

SP10

SUBSCHEMES

DISTRIBUTARY CANALS

PEAT DEPTH:
50–200 cm.
> 200 cm.
HILLY, NON-IRRIGABLE LAND
PEAT SURVEY BOUNDARY
RIVERS
PROVINCE BOUNDARY

0 1 2 3 4 5 KILOMETERS

This map was produced by the Map Design Unit of The World Bank.
The boundaries, colors, denominations and any other information shown
on this map do not imply, on the part of The World Bank Group, any
judgment on the legal status of any territory, or any endorsement or
acceptance of such boundaries.

IBRD 30501

PAPUA
NEW GUINEA

IRIAN JAYA

PACIFIC OCEAN

PHILIPPINES

AUSTRALIA

SERAM

TIMOR

INDONESIA

SULAWESI

SABAH

SARAWAK

KALIMANTAN

FLORES

BALI

MALAYSIA

BRUNEI

SINGAPORE

Java Sea

JAWA

Jakarta

SUMATERA

South China Sea

THAILAND

MALAYSIA

INDIAN OCEAN

Area of map

SP8

SP9

SP10

SUMATERA BARAT

BENGKULU

Air Manjunto

Air Manjunto

SP5

SP6

SP3

SP7

Air Pelajun

Air Hilum

Air Manjuto

INDIAN OCEAN

OCTOBER 1999

This renders the cleared, swampy fields practically useless for high-productivity paddy agriculture without major drainage works and remedial soil treatment (map IBRD 30501).

Kuamang Kuning, Jambi Province, Sumatra. About 180 displaced families moved into several of the subschemes here, but 120 families were concentrated in two subschemes. This was planned as a rainfed scheme for annual crops. The settlers got a 0.5-hectare houseplot, a cleared field of one hectare, and another one-hectare lot of forest further afield. In 1988, the transmigration authorities altered the plan, announcing that the second lots would all be planted for the settlers with oil palm, in stages, by an oil palm enterprise. By 1997 most of the subschemes have less than half their plantings and some have none. Lots that have not yet been planted must wait at least another six years for the first harvest. That means that some of the displacees who arrived in 1987 will have been waiting at least 16 years by the time they start harvesting their palm.

Bukit Saloka Village, Longikis Kecamatan, East Kalimantan. This special village absorbed 193 displaced Kedung Ombo families. The scheme comprises a nucleus palm oil estate and surrounding smallholder plantations. Each family received a 0.25-hectare houseplot, a 0.25-hectare field for food crops, and two hectares of planted palm. The palm provides them with the highest incomes of all the surveyed groups.

Nabire, Irian Jaya. Eighty-six displacees were resettled in this irrigation scheme, the earliest to receive the displacees, and the most distant location of all the Kedung Ombo transmigration sites from the reservoir. Each settler received a 0.25-hectare houseyard, one hectare of cleared and irrigated crop land, and, at a distance, another 0.75 hectare of forest waiting to be cleared. Families have done well with the irrigation scheme, while sending family members to work in a nearby expanding urban center.

Costs Are Lower Than Average

Compensation payments for displacees from the reservoir were about $30 million. Costs of transmigration of the 1,300 families transferred are estimated at $1.3 million, the equivalent of $1,000 per family. This is much lower than the $14,000 average costs per family of the typical transmigration program reported elsewhere,[7] including transport, site development, and technical support. The higher figure is a better estimator of total costs to all authorities involved in the program. Resettlement activity in the vicinity of the dam, including the new villages and some of the extension work, cost $4.2 million, and the university and other consultant work that supported RRDP cost another $2.4 million. Altogether about $55 million was spent for resettlement from the reservoir, or a little over $10,000 for each of the 5,400 displaced families. The total is about 18 percent of total project costs.[8] Most of that 18 percent was for compensation.

Land Compensation Is Too Low for Rising Land Prices and Is Not Negotiable

Compensation rates for physical assets other than land appear to have been accepted as fair. The controversy was over compensation for the different classes of agricultural land. Households were indemnified for each owned field, and many families accepted it for some fields and rejected it for others. Although compensation rates were inadequate to enable most landowners to reestablish themselves on land of similar productivity, this was not the case everywhere.

Households in the hilly areas inundated near the dam site, for example, are said to have been overpaid. Transmigrants took packages that were easily adequate to cover setup costs at the destinations. The families that accepted compensation packages early in the period, before 1986, probably found they had enough funds to reestablish an agricultural economy that matched life in the valley. Finally, families moving to Kedungmulyo got an amount of land equal to what they lost, receiving 350 rupiah per square meter for what they gave up and paying 200 rupiah per square meter for what they acquired. The difference was incorporated in the compensation package.

What the families were trading for, if they originally owned valley paddy land, was less fertile land where they had to work with more demanding cropping patterns. As is the case with all resettlement programs behind large dams, the paddy fields that are flooded cannot really be replaced at any price in the uplands surrounding the lakes. And as pressure built up, of course, prices started rising for cultivable and uncultivable agricultural land of any class. Compensation rates were wholly inadequate to accommodate the majority of displacees once they entered the market. Thus, by 1987 the recalcitrant households and NGOs were already claiming that the rates of 250 to 750 rupiah per square meters offered by the provincial government was completely out of step with market prices of reasonably good land, which was 4,000 to 5,000 rupiah per square meter. Had the government agreed to giving higher compensation to the late resettlers, it would have faced a situation where all other, as yet uncompensated, families would have stepped forward. Worse yet, it might have been impossible to avoid granting the difference to all families already paid. This was an unprecedented and, to the government, an intolerable situation.

Income Restoration Brings Higher Incomes for Many, but a Third Remain in Poverty

Nearly All Consider Themselves Better Off

In surveys of 1993 and 1997, average total family monthly incomes were estimated for the five groups of surveyed households: self-settled, in government-built villages, in the greenbelt, transmigrant, and "local." The last category served as a control.

TABLE 5.2
Monthly Family Incomes (U.S. dollars)

	1993	1996
Self-settled	47	158
In government-built villages	41	95
In greenbelt	87	73
Transmigrant		
Muko Muko	96	57
All four sites	—	117
Local (control)	54	76

—Not available.

NOTES: $1 = 2,396 rupiah. Average monthly incomes include imputed values of food products

SOURCE: 1993 incomes from Ministry of Public Works, 1994, *Socio-Economic Monitoring of Kedungombo Resettlement and Reservoir Development Program 1993,* Final Report, p. 123 (table 5.17, "June–October'93" column). The Rupiah figures have been inflated by the increase of 28 percent reported in the International Monetary Fund's Consumer Price Index 1993–1996. 1996 incomes are from Satya Wacana Christian University, Salatiga, Indonesia, *Survey of Families Displaced by the Kedungombo Dam, Now Residing Either in the Vicinity of the Reservoir or at Transmigration Sites in Sumatra, Kalimantan, and Irian Jaya,* p. 77. p. 80 (table 3.22, "Total" column).

Householders in 1997 samples of all affected groups claim they are "more prosperous" compared with the time before or right after the inundation.[9] This includes the local respondents, although they have lost ground to the self-settled and government-village respondents. The estimated incomes (table 5.2) of these two groups now surpass the local-respondent average by 109 percent and 25 percent, respectively. Despite their claim of greater prosperity, greenbelt families report income, in U.S. dollars, that is slightly lower than in 1993—falling from $87 to about $73 per family per month. The greenbelt's position relative to the other groups has deteriorated significantly.

The performance of the self-settled families has been extraordinary, and at $158 per family per month they have forged well ahead of all other groups. Government-village incomes have improved, but less rapidly than the self-settled families. Nevertheless, they, too, have passed the local-controls.

In three of the provinces, transmigrant incomes exceed the Kedung Ombo local incomes. In two cases—East Kalimantan and Irian Jaya—they exceed them by substantial margins. Only in Muko Muko are transmigrant incomes lower than the local incomes. The family monthly incomes for these groups are as follows: Irian Jaya irrigators, $186; East Kalimantan oil palm farmers, $210; Jambi food crop and oil palm farmers, $87; Muko Muko peat farmers, $66; and Muko Muko fertile farmers, $48.

An average income level for all Kedung Ombo transmigrants can be constructed by assuming that they were split equally on fertile and infertile lots at Muko Muko, and that the average income of the 769 transmigrant families lo-

TABLE 5.3
Respondents' Poverty Condition in 1996

	Percentage of poor families
Kedung Ombo	
In greenbelt	42
In government-built villages	34
Self-settled	32
Local	61
Transmigrant	
Muko Muko fertile	77
Muko Muko infertile	32
Jambi	45
East Kalimantan	0
Irian Jaya	17

cated at the four sites investigated in 1997 represents all 1,300 transmigrant families. The average for all transmigrant families would be $117.[10] This compares with $158 for the self-settled and $76 for the local families.

Income Increases Come from Diversification

Self-settled and government-village families have moved ahead of the local families partly because they have continued to expand their cultivated farmlands since 1993. The local families' cultivated landholdings, on the other hand, have been static—at three percent—with some of them selling or otherwise giving up land. These locals have been deliberately shifting their household economies from agriculture into nonfarm occupations. All the other reservoir groups have been doing the same, although the greenbelt families at a rate much slower than the others. The self-settled families have been increasing their agricultural enterprise at the same time as sending family members to outside jobs.

The shift in source of incomes is a reflection of the industrial transformation that is pulling all of Java ahead. The provincial and regency road agencies have been supporting this shift, by surfacing many of the local roads that turn off the intercity trunk roads to penetrate to communities on the edge of the lake.

Poverty Remains High after Resettlement

At least a third of responding families in all but two of the groups (transmigrants at East Kalimantan and Irian Jaya) still had incomes falling below official poverty limit for rural families, $56 per month[11] (table 5.3).

Settlers Are Satisfied with Situations and Services

In surveys of resettlers, responses to questions about adequacy of educational and health services were almost always positive, even among families living in the greenbelt, where construction of public buildings is not permitted. Of course, the *project* only provided facilities to the three government villages, while the Ministry of Transmigration provided them to the transmigration sites. Self-settled and greenbelt families depended on nonproject services.

All the new houses in the government villages were connected to the power grid, while 65 percent and 46 percent of the self-settled and greenbelt households respectively reported electric connections to their new houses (compared with 95 percent of the local families in their older houses). While all transmigrants at the Irian Jaya site, and a few in Jambi, were connected, none of the other transmigrants had electricity in their homes and depended on lanterns and candles. The water supply situation also varied. East Kalimantan transmigrant households all have connections to a piped water supply, at least as close as the yard, about 15 percent of government-village and local households have the same, and all other displacees still depend on public and private wells, springs, and rivers. The respondents were pleased with the transport services: the roads and the buses. Exceptions are the Bukit Saloka village in East Kalimantan, an isolated place, and, with respect to the access road to the camp, more distant.

Survey personnel inquired about the displaced families' sense of being "established" (*krasan* in Bahasa Indonesia), which implies stability and the intention to remain. The numbers putting themselves in this group were remarkably high across all groups—89 percent—including greenbelt families. In principle, *krasan* would not be the response of choice for a family that was still unhappy with the involuntary relocation but had no opportunity or was not allowed to leave.

The only exception was a minority of those Muko Muko farmers who had peat below their lots. Even here the attitudes were remarkably benign. In Muko Muko communities farmers spoke with optimism about the future—if not for them, at least for their children.

Government Shows Low Commitment and Uncertain Capacity

The government committed all the errors that worldwide experience indicates should be avoided in a resettlement program.

- No participation by the people living in the condemned area in planning for resettlement
- Failure to establish an institutional mechanism that can manage a large and painful exercise in social adjustment
- Compensation rates that do not acknowledge the project's effects on land prices and enable resettlers to buy substitute land assets of approximately equal earning capacity
- The worst feature of the Kedung Ombo case (highlighted by the NGO and settler protests)—the physical violence, psychological harassment, and abuse of other civil rights.

The government underfunded the program for Central Java, even after designing RRDP. Almost all of RRDP was financed by the Bank's loan. The provincial governments did not earmark extra funds for the reservoir during RRDP, and when the Bank withdrew, the resettlers lost whatever privileges they might have enjoyed.

Direct Resettler Participation Is Virtually Absent

With one exception, the resettlers were not invited to participate in any of the major decisions about compensation, relocation, and income-generating activity. Participation is a fundamental right established by Indonesian law for persons affected by government acquisition of land and other assets. Compensation rates are supposed to be agreed upon according to *musyawarah*—a process of deliberation to reach consensus—between the landowners and the party requiring the land. If the landowners are not satisfied with the outcome of the *musyawarah*, they can appeal to the courts. This process was ignored at Kedung Ombo.

Beneficiary participation in transmigration followed the conventional route, although here, too, critics maintain that the Ministry could have been more attentive to the needs of these forced relocatees and to send their leaders to inspect the prospective sites ahead of time.

Nongovernment Organizations Step In

The NGO contribution was substantial, generally beneficial, and phenomenally successful in calling attention to a situation headed toward disaster. It was shaped by confrontational advocacy, and it is doubtful that a more conciliatory posture would have been any more successful. The numbers of local and international NGOs involved in the protest was enormous, a gathering guaranteed under the leadership of the International NGO Forum on Indonesian Development (INFID). The NGOs faced mounting government hostility, and their courage deserves special recognition.

Two factors stain the NGOs' otherwise impressive record. First, militant activism by some of their field troops may have pushed the resettlers' resistance farther than they intended. Second, the NGO involvement in technical assistance to the resisting resettlers and those already relocated was not sustained beyond the first few years. In 1997, settlers complained that they felt abandoned by the NGOs.

Tensions Among Resettlers and Host Communities Is Low

The self-settlers generally moved into nearby villages where they had friends and relatives who were sympathetic to their situation. Land purchases in these host villages were governed by the land market and not by any concerted effort to limit the inflow. The only tension was between the people remaining in the greenbelt and still holding out for higher compensation[12] and those among them who elected to leave the greenbelt and move up to one of the three new government villages. When they move, they may be called traitors by those who stay, and they may be obliged to relinquish any claims to drawdown property.

By contrast, a host problem has been endemic at Muko Muko since the settlers first moved in beside the people already living in the Air Manjuto River valley. These hosts had first claim on the newly irrigated lots and left the poorer areas— including the forests that they knew were underlain by peat—to the newcomers (map IBRD 30501). Low-level tension between the hosts and the transmigrants continues.

Resettler and Nongovernment Organization Protests Change Policy

The Kedung Ombo experience led to at least two improvements in the government's position regarding involuntary resettlement. The first was a Presidential Decree issued in 1993 (No. 55/1993), that provided stronger protections and a formalized grievance system for situations calling for land acquisition. The decree also reinstates *musyawarah* as the guiding principle for negotiation and conflict resolution.

Second, compensation rates are now related to land tax rates, and, supported by Presidential Decree 55/1993, present a fairer deal to the displacees. More important, the Directorate General for Water Resources Development offers a range of resettlement options and does not promote compensation alone as the preferred option. In recent projects, displacees can select between a compensation package ("free choice"), transmigration to the islands, or "local transmigration." The last of these, wherever possible, includes rights to an irrigated lot and a house built by the authority. The irrigated lots can be in the command area downstream from the dam or other smaller irrigation schemes in the hills.

Conclusions

The project is full of lessons about the "dos" and "don'ts" of involuntary resettlement behind large dams. It also raises broader policy issues.

Field supervision is essential, particularly in the early years of project implementation. In Kedung Ombo, supervision of resettlement aspects came late, after the situation had deteriorated to the point where only salvage operations were possible.

Hands-on Bank monitoring of the process of compensation, the movement of families from the reservoir, and perhaps most important, the status of the transmigration sites should have accompanied—from the start of or even preceded by— supervision of the dam and irrigation works. Early supervision of transmigration would have revealed that the program was not attracting the families that earlier declared a willingness to go.

Under present policy and institutional constraints, transmigration is only a partial solution to involuntary resettlement problems in Indonesia. If transmigration could be targeted to specific and entire household units so that all members could transmigrate, then transmigration could be applicable; however, the receiving areas must be prepared in advance of recruitment of the people. Otherwise the displaced people will be reluctant to move or lose interest when preparations are delayed one, two, or more years as happened at Kedung Ombo. The families who joined transmigration were primarily the young, landless, or particularly land-poor villagers who had little to lose. For the others, perceived risks were much higher. Older families with multiple plots, families with children attending school, and families with part-time employment outside the reservoir had sound reasons to remain where they were, especially given the difficulty of obtaining reliable information from local authorities.

Resettler participation in planning the program, either by village representatives or in collaboration with NGOs, should have been encouraged from the start. However, it is doubtful whether the most recalcitrant of the Kemusu families would have been persuaded to abandon their positions simply by talks and transparency.

Compensation levels are always a contentious issue, and the Bank can do little more than be satisfied that the due legal process is being followed in implementing a project in which it is involved. However, any reasons to question the adequacy of the process should be addressed as a general policy issue, on a countrywide basis, before proceeding with the project. A case can be made for the Bank to intervene in setting compensation rates, at the project level and even during implementation, if government fails to react to evidence that the rates are ineffective in achieving the desired results.

The treatment of some of the transmigrants—in particular the Muko Muko peat farmers and the Jambi food-crop farmers who are still waiting after ten years for oil palm—is unconscionable. It appears that if errors are made in siting these schemes, or in establishing the production systems, the transmigrants are left to their own devices to recover. It should not have been left to an NGO, or a supervision mission on another assignment, to reveal that the largest group of Kedung Ombo transmigrants was in deep trouble.

The NGOs were indispensable in forcing the Bank to look above the dam. The ferocity of their outcry was justified. The Bank's field staff responded in force, with a broad assault on the constraints on development of the agricultural economy of the region. The RRDP was a blueprint for a local development and income policy that should have been ready from the beginning.

Still, the RRDP was not a success. It failed to induce a sense of ownership on the part of provincial and regency governments and had no success in generating budgets after the Bank's loan was closed. Further, it was less a development program than an academic study with unsustainable demonstration plots.

Whether the local authorities should have continued to give disproportionate assistance to the displacees, in preference over their much larger populations of nondisplacees at similar income levels, is an issue warranting further thought.

The Bank, by its policy, was obliged to press for exceptional treatment. The central government accepted the policy but found execution difficult. The regency governments appear to have cared little about the policy. Were they wrong, given their responsibilities to larger constituencies? One option would have been to resettle some of the displacees in the command area of the dam. Bank resettlement experts assert that that is a fair way to distribute the costs and benefits of resettlement.

Displacees on average have been able to rebuild their production systems. The self-settled families have done the best. The greenbelt families did much better than was first expected by taking advantage of the cultivable greenbelt and drawdown fields, but their relative position has slipped. There are large minorities in all groups of displacees, however, who still live in poverty. Some probably lost income because of the dam. If Bank policy were to insist that all displacees must come out at least as well as before, then averages would be the wrong indicators.

Self-settled and government-village families that have improved their income base have done so by diversifying out of agriculture. The heads of households stay on the new farms, but the older sons and daughters get jobs outside. This is a common phenomenon on Java, and in no way attributable to farsighted planning by resettlement officials. It can be argued that, if a resettlement program does not aim for diversification, yet income recovery objectives are met because of coincidental regional developments, the program cannot be considered successful.

There is general agreement that the land-for-land policy was appropriate as far as it allowed for transmigration, but that it became inoperable when applied only to areas near the reservoir.

The fact that people have to work harder after being displaced, or accept a loosening of family cohesiveness, does not render the resettlement program unsuccessful. The comfortable and relatively riskless subsistence economy in the river valleys can never be replaced and is doomed with or without a dam.

It is probable that the unanticipated potential of drawdown cultivation overtook the compensation issue in Kemusu and was overtaken in turn by opportunities for diversifying the household economy. With the exception of those greenbelt families who are reacting too slowly to the industrial revolution on Java, it could be argued that the displaced people of Kedung Ombo have moved well beyond that ugly episode.

The geopolitical elements that gave shape to the Kedung Ombo resettlement story are largely coincidental. The river that had to be dammed was the Serang. The upper reaches of the reservoir, which released a rich drawdown area annually, included the heavily populated plains of Kemusu district. These plains were inhabited by political outcasts who had reason to distrust any government development program.

Notes

1. Grobogan, Sragen, and Boyolali are regencies (*kabupaten*), administrative units immediately below the provincial level. Kemusu is actually a subdistrict (*kecamatan*), the next lower level. The "district" has effectively disappeared. It is used here for clarity and because it is commonly used in many other, similar reports.
2. In 1988, the Boyolali Regency asserted that there were 500 hard-core radicals, most of them ex-communists, living in the reservoir area in Kemusu district.
3. By March 1986, 86 percent of displaced Sragen households had accepted compensation.
4. One report in the files claims that the Legal Aid Institute had first contacted the Bank in May 1987.
5. "Nearly" is inserted to reflect the fact that the presentation is not wholly objective and unemotional. Single interviews about ugly incidents are referred to repeatedly, giving an impression of widespread and continuous outrageous behavior that is probably exaggerated. Also, the cited presentation sometimes describes events leading to potentially dangerous confrontations without saying whether or not the actual meeting was peacefully concluded. Nevertheless, the implications are clear, and it would have been difficult to describe these years of conflict without any emotion.
6. The precise figures are 2,989 farmers in the greenbelt and 2,951 in the drawdown. Of the total of 8,330 parcels, 52 percent were being farmed by the ex-owners, and the rest were under a mixture of contracts between ex-owners and cultivators and unlicensed occupation. Note that the 520 families remaining in the greenbelt were only a fraction of the number of farmers with an interest in maintaining these fields.
7. J.H. Eriksen, "Comparing the Economic Planning for Voluntary and Involuntary Resettlement," in Michael M. Cernea, (ed.), *The Economics of Involuntary Resettlement Questions and Challenges,* Washington, DC: World Bank, 1999, table 3.2, pp. 90-91.
8. Taking the project completion report figure of $282.5 million and adding another $16.9 million to account for the upward adjustment of transmigration costs.
9. University Research Institute, Satya Wacana Christian University, Salatiga, Indonesia, 1997, *Survey of Families Displaced by the Kedungombo Dam, Now Residing Either in the Vicinity of the Reservoir or at Transmigration Sites in Sumatra, Kalimantan, and Irian Jaya,* p. 77.
10. Using the numbers of transmigrants and the average incomes reported.
11. In 1997 the Bureau of Statistics' poverty limit for rural areas was set at 27,000 rupiah per capita per month, or 135,000 rupiah per family of five, or $56 at an exchange rate of 2,400 rupiah per dollar.
12. This resistance group is usually associated with six reconstituted villages in and on the edge of the greenbelt in Kemusu district, including Kedungpring.

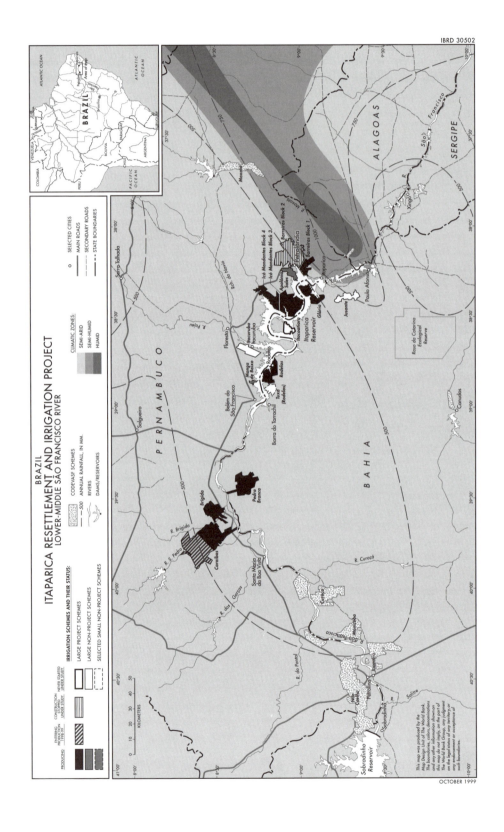

6

Good Intentions, Costly Mistakes in Brazil

The Itaparica Dam project shows sensationally how, even with good intentions by all parties, inadequate planning and failure to see the long-term consequences of short-term actions can lead to tremendous waste, without the intended benefits.

The land available for farming after the reservoir filled had poor, sandy soils and received little rain, making irrigation essential. When the Brazilian implementing agency, Companhia Hidro Eletrica do São Francisco (CHESF), realized that most affected people would not take the monetary compensation offered and migrate elsewhere, it agreed with the World Bank and Pólo Sindical do Submedia São Francisco (the farmers' union) to prepare nearby sites for irrigation. Both the agency and the Bank knew this was risky given the low-nutrient soils and high cost of irrigating these sites. Yet, although the risks were apparent, too little attention was paid to planning risk-reduction strategies.

Therefore, the agency and the Bank assumed that a primarily land-based program would suffice even for former subsistence farmers facing complex technological challenges. Insufficient estimation of the costs of land development led to funding shortfalls in the very first project year. The agency's substantial technical assistance resources have been unable to effectively provide agricultural extension or assistance in developing off-farm job skills. Not only did the project fail to ensure availability of farm credit, but it also delayed titling, which prevented farmers from obtaining credit commercially or from selling lands to others better equipped for these farming conditions.

In addition, Pólo, in its zeal to protect the farmers, forced the introduction of a monthly maintenance payment without sufficient limitations to keep it from becoming an entitlement. Each mistake caused delays. With each delay costs escalated. Between cost increases and overall government budget stringencies, time and again the agency found itself short of funds for needed resettlement infrastructure. The results: the highest resettlement costs in World Bank history, yet

TABLE 6.1
Project Chronology

Date	Event
1979	Civil works begin on Itaparica Dam.
1979	Pólo Sindical is established from seven rural labor unions to protect farmers' rights.
1985–86	Negotiations with Pólo on behalf of resettlers, often confrontational, result in agreement on rights of settlers and final package of compensation including *verba de manutenção temporária* (VMT), a temporary monthly maintenance payment.
1987, Nov.	World Bank approves Itaparica Resettlement and Irrigation Loan.
1988, Feb.	Filling of the reservoir begins.
1988, Feb.–June	Displaced families are moved to urban centers and *agrovilas*.
1988, June	Reservoir is full and power is delivered.
1988	The first small scheme receives irrigation.
1990, Feb.	World Bank approves supplemental loan to cover increased costs.
1993	Additional schemes receive irrigation.
1997, Jan.	Government Interministerial Committee is created to design the Action Plan to complete the project.
1997	2,142 lots are receiving irrigation, 1,800 lots are expected to be titled, and the remainder (1,970) are still under study.

most farmers still lack irrigation, technical know-how, and marketing channels to use their new land productively.

Short-Sightedness Leads to Increased Costs

Itaparica is one of a series of dams constructed on the São Francisco River to supply energy to the cities of northeast Brazil. The agency started civil works in 1979, closed the gates to fill the reservoir in February 1988, and started delivering power four months later (table 6.1).[1] By the mid-1980s it had become obvious that delays would aggravate an acute energy shortfall. Government and the agency were determined to maintain the construction schedule despite a late start in organizing resettlement of 8,000 families living within the perimeter of the reservoir who were unwilling to take cash compensation and leave.

The Bank did not participate in financing the Itaparica dam. As a condition for its first Power Sector Loan approved in 1986, however, it insisted that the agency plan and carry out the Itaparica rural resettlement program to meet the Bank's policy guidelines on involuntary resettlement. The Bank reinforced the agency's reluctant decision in 1985, to abandon offering only cash compensation in favor of constructing irrigation schemes that could accommodate all families that elected to stay.[2] Irrigation would create the economic base for maintaining and, "if possible," improving pre-dam living standards.

The Bank helped finance both the urban and rural components of the resettlement program.[3] The urban plans called for reestablishing the four towns in economically advantageous sites close to the lake. The rural plans were more ambitious, calling for the provision of sprinkler-irrigated lots to each of about 5,200 families (the number of families then identified), because of the inhospitable conditions for rainfed cropping on the drylands and sandy soils bordering the incised floodplain of the São Francisco. The Bank entered this complicated and risky venture convinced there was no viable alternative but concerned about the projected costs per family, the discouraging soils reports, and the limited time available to plan the enterprise before the water started rising.

To meet its schedule for filling the reservoir, the agency would have to remove all inhabitants from the reservoir site by the end of 1987. However, in May 1986 the agency had identified irrigable sites for less than half the rural population and had not started land acquisition or engineering design. With the government's promise not to close the gates until the population was safe, the Bank accepted provisional and sketchy information on sites and soils. The Bank approved the Itaparica Resettlement and Irrigation Project loan in November 1987, but within a year recognized that the costs had been underestimated. A supplemental loan was approved in February 1990.

Delays in completing the irrigation works led in 1997 to two actions: creation of a federal-level Inter-ministerial Working Group to resolve the problems, and a Request for Inspection from Pólo to the Bank's Inspection Panel. The government accepted the Working Group's Action Plan in August, obliging government to allocate $290 million to complete the program. This prompted the Bank's board to rule against an inspection.

Resettlement Requires Change from Floodplain Agriculture to Farming Land with Dry, Sandy Soils

The serpentine Itaparica reservoir is 149 kilometers long, spans 33 kilometers at its widest, and covers 840 square kilometers between the states of Pernambuco and Bahia (map IBRD 30502). It flooded 30,000 hectares of cultivated land in the valley floor, of which 8,000 hectares were irrigated by 1987. It also flooded 50,000 hectares of the thorny scrub vegetation common to the interior semiarid backlands of northeast Brazil. A small group of Tuxá Amerindians lived near the upstream end of the proposed reservoir, farming one of the larger islands.

The economy of the valley was based mostly on small farms and families of owners, tenants, sharecroppers, and landless laborers. Of the displaced rural families that were landless, 60 to 70 percent and most of the owner-operators had tenuous titles to their properties. The river determined cropping patterns: rainfall was insufficient to support intensive agriculture. The farmers practiced floodplain agriculture when the river rose during the summer wet season. When the river dropped during the dry season, they irrigated what fields they could. Yields were good, annual floods restored fertility, and no fertilizers were required. This was basically a subsistence economy, and although not comfortable, it was relatively riskless.

Thirteen large schemes were selected to accommodate most of the 5,500 rural families displaced by the dam and another 400 families displaced by the irrigation schemes (see map IBRD 30502). The group is divided first into schemes the Bank determined were viable (and therefore were included under "project" finance) and a few other large schemes in the agency's proposal that depended exclusively on government resources. The project schemes comprise two sub-groups, one close to the "lakeside" (*borda do lago*), the other made up of three "special" schemes carved out of lands 100 kilometers above the end of the reservoir. The poor quality of the soils on the higher ground next to the lake frustrated attempts to place all the families near their old homes. The special schemes had lower, more fertile lands, safe from inundation. Government also self-financed a group of smaller schemes, including integrated fish farms. The non-Bank large and small schemes absorbed about 1,400 families, compared with 4,500 under the Bank's project. The final numbers for displaced families are:

- 4,900[4] rural families eligible for an irrigated lot and (almost all of them) for a plot in an *agrovila*
- 1,000 families who moved to town but retained rights to an irrigated lot, the so-called "pararural" households
- 3,500 urban families displaced by the reservoir moved to the new urban centers
- 1,000 families who left the area, with or without a cash compensation package from the agency.

This gives a grand total of 10,400 families displaced[5] by the dam site, the reservoir, the new towns, and the irrigation schemes.

None of the schemes had good soils. Most of the lakeside schemes were on poor-to-mediocre sandy soils that were shallow and almost devoid of nutrients. Indeed, had Itaparica been approached as a discontinuous line of prospective irrigation sites, many of its lakeside schemes—or areas within schemes—would not have even been considered.

Petrolândia, a riverside community of 2,200 families and the largest "town" inundated, was entirely relocated, as were three other towns. Altogether the agency built or helped settlers to build 4,400 new houses to accommodate the previous urban populations, and the settlers themselves built several hundred more. These figures exclude those previously urban families that elected to shift to the 127 new *agrovilas* but include the rural households that elected to settle in the new towns.

Implementation of Resettlement Shows Poor Planning, with Delays Feeding Cost Escalation

The resettlement plan had two stages: first, the physical relocation of the population; and second, the development of the irrigation schemes. Stage I ranks among the most successful of any Bank-supported, large-scale relocation operation. It consisted of constructing facilities and transferring families and their possessions to four new towns and 127 *agrovilas* with roads and other public utilities, private residences, primary schools, and, in the urban centers, secondary schools and other public buildings. The agency fielded teams of social workers, agricultural agents, and field assistants to prepare the rural populations for the radical adjustment in their circumstances and to organize the transfer to the *agrovilas*. By the time the reservoir reached its operating level, all families were high and dry in new, usually better houses with electricity and running water.

Stage II consists of providing irrigation water through pressurized pipes to sprinkler systems installed on 5,900 demarcated lots ranging from 1.5 to 6.0 hectares, and totaling 20,500 hectares. More than nine years after the farmers moved into the *agrovilas* and eight years beyond the date they had been assured the schemes would be completed, this stage continues. One of the smallest schemes received water in 1988. It took until 1993 for the next group of schemes to move into production. By June 1997, about 2,100 lots (39 percent of the total on large schemes) and about 7,600 hectares were receiving water. Two other large schemes comprising 1,805 lots (34 percent) and 6,600 hectares were fully operational by the end of 1998. In May 1997, the agency foresaw that many farmers provisionally assigned to schemes still under study would have to be assigned new lots in the program or, in some cases, helped to establish other forms of livelihood. Since then, and with the approval of the Inter-ministerial Working Group's Action Plan, proposals for dealing with these farmers have developed. Some schemes (or perhaps parts of schemes) will be aborted and the farmers offered lots in other schemes (inside or outside Itaparica) or receive financial compensation.

The immediate explanations for the delay in completing the irrigation works are undisputed. The agency could not access enough Bank and counterpart funds to maintain the construction schedule because:

- The original loan of $132 million had been under-dimensioned—because of errors in predicting costs and exchange rates in Brazil's (hyper)inflationary economy.
- The energy shortage in the northeast continued and government felt obliged to concentrate funds on construction of a larger hydroelectric dam down the São Francisco River.
- The federal government simply ran out of money and could not keep up with its commitments to projects of any ranking in national priorities.
- Physical conditions within schemes were found to be less favorable for irrigation than projected and costs had to be incurred to retain the schemes or find substitutes.
- Late payment of contracts and subsequent demobilization and remobilization of contractors increased costs and exacerbated the deficit that caused the delays.

Average costs per resettled rural family (and per hectare) have jumped to extraordinary levels. The 1987 appraisal estimated costs per rural family at $37,500. In 1989, when the supplemental loan was prepared, the average costs per rural family had escalated to $63,270. By mid-1997, that figure had risen to $185,000, more than 85 percent of which had already been spent. By the same accounting, costs per irrigated hectare will reach $54,000. (Costs of the urban settlers are lower: the agency's cost estimates suggest $37,000 per family.) Costs of other irrigation schemes in the northeast have usually been $20,000 to $25,000 per family.

The total resettlement cost, about $1.5 billion, includes cash compensation and resettlement for 9,400 families that stayed and compensation for 1,000 families that left. The total cost of building the dam and power works at Itaparica is also about $1.5 billion. The one-to-one ratio of resettlement costs to dam costs is unprecedented in the Bank's portfolio. The factors that explain this outcome are

- The relatively high costs of reestablishing the community infrastructure (towns, *agrovilas*, roads, and utilities) and constructing the irrigation schemes
- The unexpected extra costs of the contracts, due to periodic demobilization, penalty clauses, and inflation adjustments
- The monthly maintenance allowances paid for the past ten years to rural families.

The agency has overarching responsibility for the resettlement operations but has assigned responsibility to Companhia de Desenvolvimento do Vale do São Francisco (CODEVASF) for managing the operating irrigation schemes. Since 1992, two groups of Brazilian and foreign technical assistance agencies have closely supported irrigating families, including the development of appropriate farming systems, and other contractors provide operation and maintenance. The delay in works in turn delayed the technical assistance. CODEVASF and the consortia have had to plan the farmer training and support programs around the late, discontinuous, and unpredictable timetable for completing individual schemes.

This study distinguished five categories of resettlers: *irrigators*, *waiters* with good prospects of receiving water, *waiters* with uncertain or poor prospects, true *urbans*, and *pararurals*. The economic conditions and prospects of these five groups are all fragile, except for the residents of Petrolândia. Even the irrigators face formidable problems. Assessing the impact of the Itaparica dam on the displaced persons must also include damage to the fabric of families and communities in all the *agrovilas*.

Compensation Gives All Displacees Land and Promises of Irrigation, but Land Titles Are Delayed

The agency surveyed the houses, shops and other urban properties, land holdings, farm infrastructure, and economic trees of the rural population. It had anticipated that 10 to 15 percent of the families would leave. Ultimately about 1,000 left—some taking cash indemnification for land and other assets lost, some receiving other benefits, and some leaving with no package. The average package for all emigrating families was approximately $5,000.

Urban resettlement gave rise to significantly fewer disputes than its rural counterpart. Homeowners had a choice. They could get freehold title to a serviced plot and construction by the agency of a new house, with both the lot and house being 20 percent larger than the originals; or they could get cash compensation for the value of existing construction plus the larger freehold plot. Those who did not own homes received title to a serviced plot and materials sufficient to construct a 55-square-meter dwelling unit. As the gate-closing deadline approached, the agency built 21-square-meter core units for all who requested them. Almost all the families moving into the four new towns occupied houses already built. Most enjoyed a substantial improvement in materials and structural integrity.

Unit values for land of different qualities and other farm assets of the families that opted for the rural resettlement program were more contentious. Pólo successfully challenged some of those initial formulas, giving the owners and users larger cash payments to supplement the resettlement package. Pólo also forced the agency to improve the standard package of benefits provided to the families in the *agrovilas*, including doubling the size of the minimum house. A 1986 agreement established the dimensions of the revised package.

- All farm families, landless as well as owners, received irrigated lots and the promise of titles within five years.
- Landless families were assigned lots of 1.5 hectares, plus increments if the number of older children and able-bodied adults exceeded certain thresholds.
- Landowners received lots of between 1.5 and six hectares, depending on the original holding, whether it was irrigated, and the size of the family.

The prevailing lot size in most schemes was three hectares, and the average holding was about 3.3 hectares. Each lot had a network of pipes feeding the sprinklers and a hookup to the distributories. All families had access to a virtual share of a common area of dryland, mostly suited to pasture.

While the displacees initially were allowed to choose between cash indemnification and the resettlement program, once they had opted for the program the agency's intention was to lock them in. A five year delay in providing title was intended to prevent speculators from prompting resettlers to make hasty sales and depart. The authorities planned to make substantial investments in technical assistance to, and training of, the original resettlers, and they wanted to protect those investments at least until the resettlers had established new production systems and could make informed judgments about likely earnings.

Lacking Means for Earning Income, Most Displacees Rely on Monthly Maintenance for Income Restoration

Temporary Subsidy Becomes Entitlement

The household monthly maintenance subsidy is a unique feature of the Itaparica program. Almost all of the rural and pararural families and some of the urban families have benefited from this *verba de manutencão temporária* (VMT). The subsidy was intended to support farmers in the transitional period between the move to the *agrovilas* starting in late 1987, and the first expected irrigated harvests a year and a half later, but the agency continues to pay the VMT to any family that once received it. The waiters depend on it, and they and the irrigators have come to treat it as an entitlement. The agency's agreement with Pólo stipulated that the VMT would be compensation for work performed by at least one adult member of each family either in clearing the bush and preparing lots for irrigation or in some other program-related activity. Pólo later shifted its position, arguing that the farmers had been promised cleared lots and therefore that the clearing and other work should be paid in cash on top of the VMT.

When the VMT was first paid in 1988, it was equivalent to 2.5 times the national minimum monthly wage, or about $100. With the increase in the real value of the national minimum wage since 1988, and, later, with a switch in the basis to the value of a basket of goods, the VMT is now worth $230. Pararurals get the same monthly check, whether they are irrigating or not and regardless of whatever other employment they have found or established in the towns.

Irrigator Incomes Improve but Are Unreliable

Farm-level analyses show that average monthly incomes for irrigating lots of three hectares are about $280, ranging from $250 at the *borda do lago* schemes to $400 at Brígida, the first of the special schemes to receive water. Brígida is unique in having established contractual relations—through help from its consortium—with agroprocessors in Petrolina to buy the whole of its October-through-November crop of industrial tomatoes.

These figures represent cash sales, and the marketing channels for almost all crops grown at Itaparica are unorganized and insecure. The way farmers choose crops for coming seasons is described as a "lottery." Marketing channels usually depend on traders who buy at the farm gate.[6] Even the Brígida success with tomatoes is vulnerable. That scheme can only count on another three or four years before it will have to abandon tomatoes in the face of accelerating pest infestation and rising costs, a life-cycle profile common to all tomato success stories. Access to these schemes has always been difficult and has recently deteriorated because of poor physical road conditions and the threat of assaults along some roads, further restricting the marketability of surplus crops.

Other sources of income for rural families are pensions, which figured in the household economies of about half of irrigators interviewed, sales of livestock products, sales of produce from farm holdings outside Itaparica, and off-farm and nonfarm earnings. Noticeably missing from almost all family income profiles are remittances from migrant family members working outside Itaparica. The Itaparica families assert that absent members typically do not send significant amounts of money home. Often the flow is in the other direction.

Average monthly cash incomes for the three hectare farmers are thus about $420, or $650 with the VMT. Comparisons suggest that the Itaparica families are relatively privileged. Average predam monthly cash income of 95 percent of all rural families threatened by the dam was less than the equivalent of $100. The minimum salary throughout Brazil was about $104 (raised to the present equivalent of $109 in May 1997). Yet most farmers are anxious about their future in the schemes, concerned about the impact on their income of gradual reduction of the VMT and the eventual requirement to assume operation and maintenance costs. Many would leave if they could.

Yields are decreasing on all schemes. Although this phenomenon is common on projects that open new lands, at Itaparica it is exceeding previous projections and is irreversible in the absence of a substantial build-up in fertilizer usage and improvements in crop husbandry. Manure and inorganic fertilizers (both are required) are expensive in Itaparica. Present yields and incomes are too low to justify large expenditures on purchased inputs even with credit.

Many scheme soils are highly prone to salinization, due to the high salt content of the river water intercepted for irrigation and the rapid rate of evaporation in this climate. Drainage and better water management are essential, but the drainage program is in its infancy.

Farmers do not yet pay for irrigation water. Most Itaparica schemes have exceptionally high costs in energy consumed to deliver water from the São Francisco River through the pressurized sprinkler systems. The Bank and the agency believe that water tariff rates may require permanent subsidy, and the Action Plan accepts that position. The Bank now insists, however, that irrigators begin assuming at least part of the operation and maintenance costs.

Any definitive improvement in farm incomes under the fragile conditions at Itaparica will depend on outstanding technical performance by the farmers. Regardless of whether the majority of these displacees can ever rise to that level of technical performance, the sustainability of this first wave of settler families in the Itaparica perimeter will depend upon what the children decide to do. The enforced idleness of the teenagers and young adults, the years they missed from hands-on farm experience, and their exposure through schooling in town to nonfarm activities and Brazil's jeans and *novela* culture suggest that the majority may reject farming these lots and their $280 monthly incomes.

These grim realities are offset by favorable factors that could rescue many schemes provided they are farmed by competent, motivated persons with access to credit and other institutional support. Even the sandy soils will respond to good management of nutrients and appropriate cropping patterns. To prevent land sales that would help ensure effective matching of farming skills with land assets is neither realistic nor feasible over the long run.

Cropping conditions on the special projects are not significantly inferior to those on large schemes near Petrolina.[7] These schemes include large enterprises as well as small farms in the six to eight hectare range. All these schemes have experienced a continuous turnover of small-lot holders. The turnover accelerated in the early 1990s when farmer organizations began to charge their members the full cost of water. Approximately 70 percent of the original irrigators (not involuntary resettlers) have been replaced. Technical skills have improved, and a reasonably competent farmer with a six hectare lot should be able to clear $2,000 per month, comparable to $1,000 on three hectares. That is almost four times the present average earning from the lots at Itaparica ($280).

In principle, the lot holders at Itaparica are unable to sell their lots, although informal sales take place. The agency is now accelerating the titling process. By September 1996, 1,800 of the 5,800 lots had been titled and the agency hoped to complete 70 percent by the end of 1997. One reason the agency is pushing is to give the farmers security to apply for credit. This push will also result in an increase in the rate of sale. Although many farmers refuse to accept their titles until the agency has provided all the agreed resettlement benefits, they might change that attitude if there was an open market for lots. The future of the special schemes and parts of the lakeside schemes would be transformed if the process of turnover common in the schemes upriver gathers momentum at Itaparica. Some predict that Itaparica will ("can only") evolve in exactly the same direction, implying that most of the present families will eventually leave.

Waiter Incomes Depend on Temporary Subsidies

Without income from an irrigated lot, the waiters depend much more on the VMT. The waiters, like the irrigators, count on non-lot cash incomes of about $140. Most waiters reported household from dryland cropping—mainly beans and maize with some melon. As with the irrigators, waiters' income from remittances was negligible. The waiters are worse off than the average rainfed farmers in these two states because they live inside the *scrubland* and if they cultivate at all, they cultivate poorer soils. It is unlikely that the crops they manage to harvest are sufficient to feed the family; thus, they have to use the VMT to buy basic foodstuffs.

Urban Incomes Vary from Town to Town

A survey of urban resettlers in Petrolândia and Itacuruba, the two new towns in Pernambuco, revealed striking differences. In Petrolândia, 30 of the 34 interviewed families had established secure income streams from their own businesses or from wage earnings. Only three of the 34 receive the VMT.[8] The average monthly earnings of these households were about $460 (excluding the VMT).

In Itacuruba, only eight of the 20 interviewed families had secure off-farm income streams. However, 18 received the VMT and, like the waiters, depended on it. Almost as soon as the project started, a proposed irrigation scheme nearby was declared nonviable and construction work was aborted. Nevertheless, the agency continues to carry the Itacuruba residents on its rolls as pararurals.[9] Apart from the VMT, average cash incomes were about $165.

Pararural Incomes Are Based on Nonfarm Jobs and Temporary Subsidies

Of 20 pararurals in Petrolândia, all but three families had been assigned lots and were still waiting for water. As their assigned lots are likely to get water eventually, this group corresponds to the waiters with good prospects for irrigating. All pararurals get the VMT. In addition, most of those interviewed had developed other income sources. Their average monthly income of $430 is almost as high as their "urban" counterparts, but because they also get the VMT, they enjoy a particular advantage with respect to all other groups at Itaparica. The soils of the lots are bad, however; so the prospective irrigation conditions of most pararurals in the Itaparica program are worse than those of the irrigators. That disadvantage is offset by their success in establishing lines of urban employment.

Indigenous Groups Are Worse Off than Pararurals

The Tuxá Amerindians have fared poorly. The community of about 190 families living in and near Rodelas split into two groups of almost equal size following a partisan political dispute. One group moved to a distant site where they received homes and the promise of 200 hectares of irrigated land and 2,000 hectares of rainfed farmland. The other group remained near the lake, moving into new homes in a separate neighborhood on the outskirts of the new Rodelas town. They were promised an irrigated site of 100 hectares and another 4,000 hectares of dryland nearby. Both groups are complaining. The land assigned to them proved inappropriate for irrigation, and it has taken three years to identify and agree on a substitute site. Until then, this group of Tuxá is listed among the rest of the waiters, nine years after shifting to their homes. Unlike the pararurals who are also waiting for irrigated lots, the Tuxá find it harder to secure substitute urban jobs.

Organized and Spontaneous Income-Generation Activity Is Lacking

A distinguishing feature of the Itaparica experience is that the agency has so far sponsored no organized activity, other than the irrigation schemes, to enhance resettler incomes. Urban resettlers have been left to their own devices since the initial move. The idle families in the waiting *agrovilas* similarly have been left to manage on the VMT and otherwise fend for themselves.[10]

During project preparation, the Bank had promoted development of the lake's fishery. In addition, the agency pressed ahead with plans for a form of fish farming (*piscigranjas*) that uses artificial ponds just off the lake and integrates the management of fish, hogs, and ducks in a symbiotic system. After implementation started, both the fishery and fish-farming initiatives stalled. Nothing appears to have been done to train and finance idle resettlers to move into capture fishery (although many of them had fished part-time on the river before the dam). Nor have cages or pen enclosures in the small bays been discussed. The agency built four communities of fish farms, but for various reasons they all failed. Eight years that could have been used to advance this secondary occupation have been wasted.

Social Services Improve But Are Less than Promised

The rural resettlement program called for adequate education and health facilities to serve the *agrovilas*. Altogether 67 lower primary schools (grades one through four) were built in the 127 *agrovilas*. The agency has provided bus services to nearby towns for the older primary school children and for all high school students. The schools are integrated into the state school systems and suffer the same shortages that are common throughout the rural areas. Teacher entry qualifications are high, most successful candidates are from the towns, and many seek transfers out of the *agrovilas* as quickly as possible.

Fifteen health "posts" were established in the *agrovilas* and the three special schemes were each given a larger health "center." These temporary posts were intended to be replaced with larger facilities at scheme centers, but most of the sites for those centers have yet to be developed.

The biggest deficit in the social infrastructure lies in the community centers that had been planned for each scheme. The community centers combine the higher primary school, the health center, other public buildings, markets, parks, and recreational areas in a convenient centralized block. Eight were planned, none have been completed, and most have not even been started.

Resettlers Fear the Future but Want to Move

Judging by the actions of the families and their answers to questions asked in interviews and other discussions, few resettlers are satisfied (except in Petrolândia), many are insecure and uncertain of a satisfactory outcome, and a large minority are convinced that their conditions and prospects have deteriorated. With some exceptions, they agree that their homes are better built and welcome the hook-ups to public utilities. A high percentage of families has a range of durable household assets, particularly in the towns. Most families in all schemes and towns noted improvements in the level and quality of such public services as health facilities, schools, water quality and sanitation, post, transport, and the like, although many resettlers expressed reservations over the quality of school and health facilities.

Apart from their attitudes about homes and services, the rural resettlers have widely different views about incomes earned and expected. In a 1997 survey of 121 irrigators, 34 percent said they would sell their properties and move away if they were allowed to do so, including 43 percent of those from Brígida, the pearl of the program. The same sort of question of 71 waiters found 59 percent optimistic and 22 percent negative.

The survey data are not the only strong indicators of resettler ambivalence toward the progress of the Itaparica program. Pólo and its members are trying to get the agency and the Bank to stay involved until the economy of the irrigation works is secured. The agency identifies six "boiling caldrons" where resettler unhappiness is bubbling over: three of the waiting irrigation schemes, two of the low-income towns, and the Tuxá Indian community. By keeping passions high, Pólo contributes to the negative attitude, although it is quick to step in to restrain the farmers when it feels the confrontations with the agency get too rough.

An important task now is to wean the irrigators off the VMT and remove the dependency factor. A cutoff is bound to be traumatic. Even with the VMT, these families are not rich, and loss of the subsidy will cut into expenditures now deemed essential. This is supported by a 1996 survey done to determine what would be a "minimum" income level to maintain the rural resettlers at their present standard of living. The "minimum" income level turned out to be $540 per month, almost five times the minimum salary. If the agency had been able to withdraw the VMT in 1989, as planned, the dependency could have been avoided. Nine years later it is too late. It appears that unless the authorities are able to stabilize the earnings from irrigated farming at a level twice as high as at present ($280), any precipitous action on the VMT risks a violent reaction.

Government Shows Commitment

Government deserves applause for continuing to support this operation even while costs were expanding far beyond original estimates. The delays in construction attributable to funding shortfalls were due not to government's refusal to invest the funds agreed at appraisal but to its inability to keep up with endless demands for supplementary allocations. Government commitment is responsible for bringing the project as far as it has come.

At first, the agency management preferred cash compensation for all displacees. The agency's conversion to the increasingly expensive irrigation program has remained ambivalent. Under pressure from Pólo, the agency had already decided on irrigation when the Bank entered the scene in 1985. The Bank's moral support emboldened Pólo to raise its conditions, however, forcing the agency to concessions it may not have otherwise made.

The ten year delay in completing the irrigation works (1988–98) is the most damaging factor undermining whatever prospects this project might have had.

Had the schemes been completed with only a short delay, government implementers could have turned in unison to concentrate their attention on the factors essential to production success: extension, soils, credit, and markets. Government's failure to provide the funds to comply with the agreed schedule of *works* must bear the most blame for the "boiling caldrons," and the other ugly consequences of the Itaparica program.

Another weakness in government participation relates to the credit component. The government maintained in 1987 that normal sources would provide farm credit. As government lines of farm credit dried up throughout the northeast, this did not happen. Proper farm development at Itaparica depended on credit, since most of the families arrived without savings or compensation packages. That deplorable situation began to improve in 1997. The Bank of Northeast Brazil started to enter the schemes with group credits (for individual members but guaranteed by the group) earmarked for specific enterprises. Once the agency hands the irrigators their lot titles, these can provide the collateral for funding individuals directly.

The experience at Itaparica has not prompted any significant modification of the federal government's policies and instructions on resettlement. Itaparica is considered a unique tragedy. Federal and state implementing agencies continue to develop a resettlement strategy piecemeal, scheme-by-scheme. However, planners and managers at other schemes in Brazil, especially in the northeast, are aware of the unfortunate developments at Itaparica and have shaped their work to avoid similar problems.

Pólo's Power as the Representative of Displacees Leads to Problems

Pólo Sindical, established in 1979 from seven local, rural labor unions and headquartered in Petrolândia, emerged in the mid-1980s as a powerful advocate for the families threatened by the dam and other project works. Pólo is a "workers" syndicate, Brazilian terminology for a representative farmer organization. The organization's main objective was to protect Itaparica farmers from injustices. Although in 1997 less than half of agrovila and pararural families are formal members of the local unions comprising Pólo, almost all consider Pólo their legitimate representative. Resettler "participation" is wholly described by the activities of Pólo. No other channels for farmer involvement have existed, and none were thought necessary.[11] Apart from the periods of confrontation, Pólo has taken a responsible position with respect to finding solutions to Itaparica's problems.

Pólo led the protest movement that gathered momentum in 1985. The agency's work on the dam continued unabated, without any serious action on resettlement plans and only two years before the gates were scheduled to close. Pólo gained extra strength from the obvious sympathies of the Bank for resettler interests. The confrontation with the agency and government led to a widely publicized invasion of the agency's construction site at the Itaparica dam in November

1986. This in turn led to the agreement signed on December 6, 1986, which defined the rights of the resettlers, committed the agency to accelerate resettlement preparations, and obliged Pólo to leave the site and avoid violence. Although subsequently adjusted and expanded, that December agreement became the basis for the final package of compensation, transfer, and settlement rights.

According to some, Pólo's influence on that package pushed "participation" too far, and in excess it became dysfunctional. The rural resettler package Pólo gained is widely considered (but not by Pólo or the farmers) too generous, including larger lots, larger houses, the amount of the VMT, and especially, the transformation of the VMT from a wage to a grant. Local influences and worker representation in the mid-1980s were irresistible forces, however. Brazil's military government had lost control in 1985, and the liberal government that replaced it was sympathetic to the resurgence of popular movements.

Pólo's primary platform—the insistence on a land-for-land resettlement package near the lake for all displacees—in hindsight was intransigent and unsound. The shift to high-tech irrigation systems on soils that Pólo knew were risky was not a sensible solution for a large number (perhaps a majority) of Pólo's constituency.

The preceding paragraphs mainly refer to participation by the rural resettlers. Participation by the urban resettlers in town-site selection and town design was organized by the agency and carried out satisfactorily. Alternative sites were discussed and voted on at community meetings.

Other Nongovernmental Organizations Show Only Sporadic Interest

Pólo is sometimes described as an NGO, so in that sense NGO involvement has been decisive. Apart from Pólo and the organization that carried out surveys, NGOs have played an occasional, challenging, and usually distant role at Itaparica. An NGO-orchestrated flood of protest letters flowed into the Bank and Itaparica in October 1986 to support Pólo's appeal to the agency for immediate action. Oxfam was instrumental in that campaign. Five months later, after the December agreement, another wave of look-alike letters congratulated the Bank's task manager for having helped resolve the dangerous situation. Subsequently, the international community of NGOs only rarely addressed the Bank about the problems of Itaparica. The Bank's September 1997 decision not to approve a formal inspection prompted immediate protests from several international NGOs.

Conclusions

The siting, design, and extent of the irrigation program were driven more by lending factors and global resettlement strategies than by conditions on the ground or by a broad vision of the departees as "beneficiaries" of a national development program. The result is an expensive program whose opportunities are of mixed value to the departees.

Recovery projects should be designed to suit the character of the beneficiaries.

Few of the resettled families were technically qualified or experienced commercial farmers. However, to develop a viable commercial farm economy in the new schemes farmers will have to convert from floodplain agriculture that is low input and low output to sprinkler irrigation regimes. Furthermore, they will have to do so on relatively unproductive (although viable) soils demanding expensive organic and inorganic fertilizers and a cocktail of pesticides without guarantee of recovering expenses on any particular crop. A period of self-selected culling of the uninterested families seems inevitable, putting the viable lots in the hands of persons who want to learn to work them and manage their markets. Such a turnover process, associated with some concentration of land holdings, is exactly what the project hoped to avoid. In the end, most displaced families will probably migrate.

The costs of this program are extraordinary, providing only a model of what not to do. At $185,000 per resettled rural family on the schemes, $54,000 per hectare, and almost a one-to-one ratio between costs of resettlement and costs of the dam and power plant, the costs of this operation far exceed those for any other involuntary resettlement program. Irrigating families that cost $185,000 to relocate are now clearing less than $3,000 per year from their lots.

This outcome would have been less likely if the Bank and the agency had designed an effective compensation package. At $5,000, the average actual payment to the 1,000 families that left at the beginning was a fraction of the expenditures on the 9,400 families that stayed. $5,000 is not a valid cost estimate for a well-conceived compensation option. Nevertheless, a cash compensation package that included "relocation assistance" clearly would have been much cheaper than the route taken.

The ten year delay in installing irrigation infrastructure is partly responsible for the explosive conditions in some of the *agrovilas* and towns, but it is not the basic reason for the failure of Itaparica to reach its objectives. The fundamental problem was that the land-for-nearby-land strategy, implemented with replacement lots of marginal quality (combined with restrictions on land sale), flew in the face of agronomic as well as economic logic. Itaparica was not viewed as an opportunity for a broad-based regional development program, taking imaginative advantage of all the assets created, including the reservoir. People sit idle in some of the towns and *agrovilas*, and no organized attempt is being made to give them alternative productive employment. Too little attention was given to marketing the produce from the irrigated lots, except by desperate farmers and opportunistic buyers.

The job now is to absorb the lessons of failure and adopt a bolder approach to resolving the problem. The Bank intends to continue its supervision of this project for two years beyond closing the loan. The program, however, has at least another six years of life because lot owners receiving irrigation for the first time in 1998 (maybe the last to get it) are promised technical assistance for another five years. The preparation of a viable design is as exciting a challenge as any facing the Bank. That design should:

- Help the settlers who want to remain to achieve remunerative cropping systems
- Control the inevitable process of self-culling and turnover and try to limit the equally inevitable process of concentration to operations with high rates of employment
- Actively assist those families who elect to sell and leave to establish household economies elsewhere.

The most delicate issues within the overall solution are the handling of the VMT and the recovery of water charges. Because the VMT has been converted from a short-term palliative into a permanent component of the families' household economies, it would be prudent to schedule removal of the VMT in tandem with the establishment of a reliable high-input, high-output farming system.

Likewise, the water charges should be applied only when and if the lots can sustain them. The agency should not be too generous with its clients. The resettlers should be given the tools to manage their irrigation systems and production so that they can successfully manage the risks to which they are normally exposed.

The experience at *Itaparica shows how important it is to refine the overall policy goal of improving "incomes."* What should be stressed is neither incomes (the VMT solves nothing) nor short-term cash earnings (the Brìgida tomato bonanza will not last). Rather, the goal should be to create opportunities for sustained, substantial remuneration for productive employment.

Pólo clearly had a profound influence on farmers, the agency, government, and the Bank. That its mission was compromised by an ill-suited objective narrows the room for praise, but it does not detract from Pólo's remarkably professional performance as a leader of an unorganized peasantry.

Notes

1. The dam is 105 meters high, 4.7 kilometers long, and forms a reservoir covering 840 square kilometers. The power plant (Luiz Gonzaga Hydroelectric) has an installed capacity of 1,500 megawatts, comprising six units of 250 megawatts, and a planned capacity of 2,500 megawatts.

2. Companhia Hidro Eletrica do São Francisco technical staff favored irrigation and other income-generating schemes for Itaparica. CHESF's leadership, which preferred cash compensation, ultimately accepted irrigation.

3. When Bank staff presented the Power Sector Project to the Board in June 1986, they promised that the Bank would participate in the Itaparica resettlement operation.

4. This figure is approximate. The agency's own accounts differ, and differ also from Bank accounts, mostly for the small schemes.

5. A few families assigned to CHESF's small schemes lost land but not their homes.

6. Fundaj's surveys show that tomatoes and melons are grown mostly for sale and sold at the farm gate; onions are also grown mostly for sale and carried to markets to sell; beans are grown mostly for home consumption; and the rest are sold at the farm gate, except for maize, which is almost all consumed at home.

7. The study mission visited three schemes: Nilo Coelho, Maniçoba, and Curaça (map IBRD 30502).

8. It is uncertain why these three do, since the urban resettlers were ineligible for it.

9. On some of its tables, CHESF continues to list an irrigation scheme with 271 lots for Itacuruba "under study." On other lists it has been deleted. The Working Group included it in its scope of study.

10. One partial exception is recent work by consortia field staff to increase exploitation of the resettlers' traditional dryland enterprises, such as goat herding.

11. At least by supporters of Pólo. Others have argued that Pólo's representations may not have accurately reflected the desires of the average family facing displacement, and a truly participatory process never took place. The study did not investigate the divergence of Pólo and displacee interests.

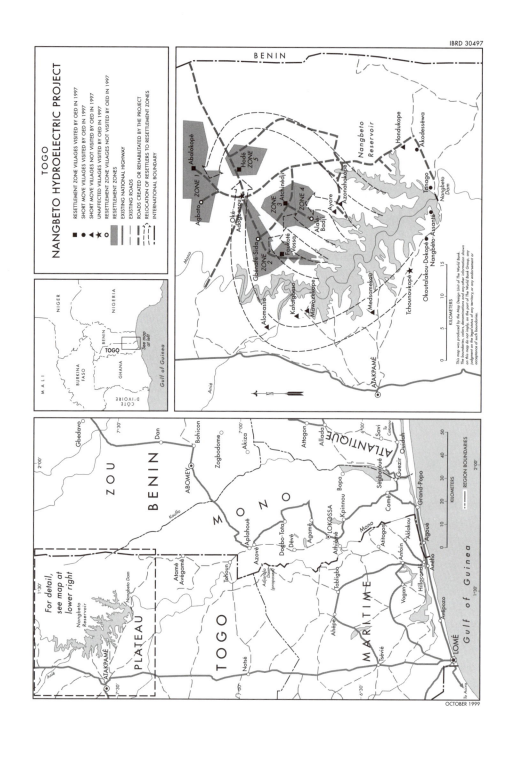

TOGO
NANGBÉTO HYDROELECTRIC PROJECT

RESETTLEMENT ZONE VILLAGES VISITED BY OED IN 1997
SHORT MOVE VILLAGES VISITED BY OED IN 1997
SHORT MOVE VILLAGES NOT VISITED BY OED IN 1997
UNAFFECTED VILLAGES VISITED BY OED IN 1997
RESETTLEMENT ZONE VILLAGES NOT VISITED BY OED IN 1997
RESETTLEMENT ZONES
EXISTING NATIONAL HIGHWAY
EXISTING ROADS
ROADS CREATED OR REHABILITATED BY THE PROJECT
RELOCATION OF RESETTLERS TO RESETTLEMENT ZONES
INTERNATIONAL BOUNDARY

IBRD 30497

BENIN

Nangbéto Reservoir

ZONE 1   ZONE 5
Abalokopé   Hodé
Agbato   Atchinédji
Oké-   ZONE 3   ZONE 4
Adingagnon   Ayoro   Azonahokopé
Gbénafié-Sida   Alofé
ZONE 2   Bodji   Tanogo
Alomassia   Epakoté   Nangbéto
             Yossa   Dam
Katafighaso
Mawozétope   Okoutalakou-Dokopé
          Medsamekoti   Nangbéto-Assanta
                          Tchounoukopé
Mono   Hondukopé
Anié   Akodesséwa

ATAKPAMÉ

KILOMETERS
0   5   10   15

This map was produced by the Map Design Unit of The World Bank.
The boundaries, colors, denominations and any other information shown
on this map do not imply, on the part of The World Bank Group, any
judgment on the legal status of any territory, or any endorsement or
acceptance of such boundaries.

N

MALI
NIGER
BURKINA FASO
NIGERIA
BENIN
TOGO
CÔTE D'IVOIRE
GHANA
See map at left
Gulf of Guinea

ZOU
BENIN
Gbedavo   Dan
                 Bohicon
        Zogbodome   Akizo
ABOMEY
Kouffo
MONO
        Aplahoué
Atomé-
Avégamé   Doğbo-Tota
        Azové   Dévé   Agamé   LOKOSSA
Tohoun   Athiémé   Kpinnou
Adjralla Dam   Bopa
(proposed)   Tabligbo   Comé
For detail,   Anfoin
see map at   Aklakou
lower right   MARITIME Vogan   Hillacondji
Nangbéto   Avépozo
Reservoir   Notsé   Ahépé
Nangbéto Dam   Tsévié
Anié   LOMÉ
ATAKPAMÉ   PLATEAU
TOGO   Aného
                    Gulf of Guinea
To Accra

ATTOGON   Allada   Savi   To Cotonou
                   Ouezir   Ouidah
        Ségbohoué   Grand-Popo
ATLANTIQUE

KILOMETERS
0   10   20   30   40   50

REGION BOUNDARIES

OCTOBER 1999

7

Resettlement without Rehabilitation
in Togo

Togo's Nangbeto Dam illustrates the importance of understanding and articulating program objectives for resettler rehabilitation and income restoration right from the start. The Togolese government's implementing agency performed beautifully in planning and executing relocation of displaced families; however, once the relocation was proclaimed a success, it considered the job done. With this short-term perspective, the government failed to consider longer-term issues that would affect the livelihood of resettlers: for example, the likelihood that improved infrastructure would attract immigration, causing increased pressures on the land; and the need to ensure access to agricultural inputs if farmers were to crop intensively. Lacking a long-term view, the government could adopt fuzzy, vacillating policies towards land tenure, tree compensation, fishing rights and other issues without worrying about their long-term consequences. It saw no need for a monitoring system to assess progress in rehabilitation. This allowed conditions to deteriorate in the resettled areas without ringing alarm bells that might trigger corrective actions.

A situation that project planners couldn't have corrected made matters even worse: political upheaval and economic collapse of the Togolese economy. Not only did this render the government incapable of heeding Nangbeto resettlement problems for two years or more, but it makes it difficult now to separate the effects of lack of long-term resettlement planning at Nangbeto from the effects of overall economic decline. That complicates any future effort at correcting past deficiencies. Since incomes declined both for displacees and villagers unaffected by the project, belated efforts to rehabilitate resettlers are likely to draw criticisms by unaffected villagers of inequitable treatment. It raises the question of just how much responsibility for income restoration the implementing agency should make in a situation of overall economic decline.

TABLE 7.1
Project Chronology

Date	Event
1980	Government of Togo begins planning on Nangbeto dam site.
1984, Jan.	The World Bank project is approved.
1985, Nov.	The project authority appoints permanent resettlement officer.
1996–98, Jan.	Food aid is provided to ease resettlement transition.
1987	Relocation takes place smoothly over five months.
1990	Final compensation payments are made.
1990	National political crisis and economic collapse, plunging the entire country into decline.
1993, Dec.	Implementation Completion Report published.
1995	The economy begins to recover.
1997	Resettler problems at Nangbeto are discovered.

A Clear Definition of Income Restoration Is Needed

Nangbeto is the first hydropower project in Togo. The Mono River is 530 kilometers long—the last 80 kilometers before it flows into the Gulf of Benin form the border between Benin and Togo—and has a catchment area of 15,680 square kilometers. The Nangbeto site—160 kilometers upstream of the coast and entirely inside Togo—is the only place where a dam of sufficient volume to regulate the Mono River flow is possible (see map IBRD 30497).[1] The reservoir and resettlement areas are entirely within Togo, but the power is shared with Benin, through the binational power company, Communauté Electrique du Bénin (CEB). The World Bank's assistance was approved on June 28, 1984 and the project ended on June 30, 1992 [2] (table 7.1).

Ten Thousand People Are Displaced from a Wide Valley

Nangbeto is a composite dam with a 4.4–kilometer-long, earth-filled lateral dike and a central rockfill section 500 meters long and 40 meters high. The reservoir, covering 180 square kilometers, lies in a flat, broad valley, so small changes in its elevation flood large parcels of land. The powerhouse contains two turbines of 31.5 megawatts each. Nangbeto has one of the lowest ratios of hydropower to land flooded or people resettled of any dam in the world.

The dam and reservoir affected 34 villages and approximately 10,600 people. Twenty-one of the affected villages closest to the river, containing 7,626 people, lost their houses and land. These people were relocated 10 to 30 kilometers from existing settlements to nine new villages in five "resettlement zones" (map IBRD 30497) northeast of the Nangbeto Reservoir ("resettlement zone" resettlers). Several former villages were consolidated into each resettlement village, with the people's consent, because it was cheaper and easier to build roads and community infrastructure for fewer, larger villages. Another ten villages containing 3,000 people ("short move" resettlers) lost mainly their houses and moved a few kilometers back from the river to make space for the reservoir. They continued to farm their previous fields. Finally, three villages totaling 1,400 people were excessively isolated by the reservoir, so new access roads were built to those villages, making their resettlement unnecessary.

The Initial Success of Resettlement Implementation Is Erased by Unforeseen Hardships

The project was approved without much resettlement planning. It gave no indication of where the resettlers might move, what they would do when they got there, or any other arrangements. Even the estimated number of affected people— 8,000—was 25 percent below the actual number.[3] Since it would be three more years before the reservoir would begin to fill, there was no compelling need to work on resettlement. Nevertheless, CEB met the target date of end-1985 for providing the detailed resettlement plan. CEB began preparations in the field in early-1986 using a highly participatory approach.

The actual relocation was expeditious and smooth. Relocation began in January 1987, after resettlers harvested their crops in December, and 7,600 "resettlement zone resettlers" were relocated in two months, in time to prepare fields for the next crop. The short-move resettlers were relocated over the next three months. There was no force, coercion, adverse incident, or hostile reaction. Food aid was provided from January 1986 to January 1988 to ease the transition. CEB provided new, quasipermanent, two-room core houses, and compensation for acquired houses so resettlers could finish new houses according to their needs and standards. The resettlement zone area was sparsely populated, and the soils were fresh and provided relatively good yields. There was little problem obtaining adequate land from host communities. CEB built good laterite access roads to the resettlement villages, which gave them unprecedented marketing opportunities. Schools, health clinics, drinking water systems, and other community infrastructure were provided at higher standards than for most of Togo. It is easy to understand why resettlement was perceived to be satisfactory at the time.

However, resettlement cannot be completed two months after people move; in that time resettlers are just beginning to adjust to their new lives. The project had conceptualized resettlement as limited more or less to the construction of the physical infrastructure and the transfer of the affected population from their homeland to the new resettlement zones. Land was allocated on the basis of holdings the resettlers exploited. The land tenure system was left ambiguous as CEB and the Government of Togo made no legal or quasilegal allocation, but preferred to leave land tenure up to traditional chiefs. Furthermore, "allocations based on exploitation" presumably refers to land currently under cultivation, but people in the Nangbeto area practiced extensive agriculture and depended on having secure access to five times as much land as they had under cultivation.

Since the project did not provide all the land resettlers needed, land pressure has increased. Unfortunately, no monitoring and evaluation of progress was carried out. The situation worsened without anyone noticing, so nothing was done.

Conditions for resettlers, and most Togolese, deteriorated precipitously after 1990, when the government was nearly overthrown. The entire economy collapsed: the government ceased to provide many services; a general strike paralyzed the country for most of 1993; the 1994 currency devaluation made conditions worse; and incomes fell dramatically until 1995, when the economy gradually began to recover. The Bank program in Togo was dormant from 1992 to 1995, and there was no Bank dialogue with the government. Because the situation deteriorated for nonresettlers as well as resettlers, it is difficult to disaggregate the effects of resettlement from the broader effects of Togo's economic decline.

Several other factors make it difficult to evaluate resettlement performance at Nangbeto. There was no baseline information, no monitoring or evaluation, and no survey data. There were no NGOs (or other third party observers) during the relocation and the early years of rehabilitation that would have been useful sources of information. The situation is extremely complicated, with some villages doing much better than other villages, and some resettlers doing well even in villages where most resettlers appear to be in difficulty. For all these reasons, conclusions must necessarily be tentative. "Resettlement zone resettlers" have not fared well. Most water supply pumps failed repeatedly and were too costly to maintain. When nearby host villages did not receive new water systems, they began using the resettlers' water systems and contributed to their deterioration. The schools and clinics often lack supplies and staff, and medicines are no longer subsidized. The core (replacement) houses, intended only for temporary occupancy, were not well constructed; many were built on shifting soil and developed cracks or collapsed. Many of the older resettlers did not adjust to life in the new village: some died, perhaps for psychological as much as for physical reasons. Most resettlers report declining agricultural yields, per capita production, and income.

There are several reasons for the agricultural decline. The benefits of the resettlement program—development of the reservoir fishery and the road system—attracted inmigration. Increased population density made it impossible to sustain the former extensive agricultural system where household landholdings averaged 16 hectares of land, only two to three hectares of which were farmed in any one year, with land left fallow for seven to ten years. People had little choice but to adopt a more intensive agricultural system, resulting in increasing exhaustion of the soil. Most resettlers cannot afford fertilizers, improved seeds, and other inputs to maintain productivity.

As land pressure increased, the host villages became increasingly reluctant to give resettlers access to land. Resettlers are unable to obtain sufficient land to farm, and what they do get is often the less desirable land. It is usually not contiguous with their villages or other plots, so raising livestock is difficult and has generally declined. Resettlers do not feel secure enough to plant trees because they might not reap the benefits. The host communities were never offered any incentives for accepting the resettlers. CEB claims it never committed to doing anything more than hand over responsibilities after relocation; but with no clear responsibility for follow-up, such an unsustainable resettlement strategy was excessively risky.

Short-move resettlers fared no better. While they have more secure land rights, they also suffer greater land pressure and soil exhaustion problems. The reservoir inundated some of their land, and finding replacement land is very difficult. Very few of them take advantage of fishing opportunities in the reservoir. They attempt to practice drawdown agriculture, but hippopotamuses eat crops in the drawdown area. The reservoir has become a premier reserve for thousands of hippos that are protected by stiff fines and jail terms for those who harm them.

Not all resettlers are suffering. Some "resettlement zone" villagers say their old land was already exhausted and they are better off now. They used to grow rustic (unimproved) cotton, but inputs and marketing supplied by the national cotton parastatal have improved the quality and cotton now provides the main cash crop.[4] Those who are able to afford improved inputs and to sell their crops at the time of their choice (that is, not right at harvest time when many other farmers are trying to sell) realize much higher yields and prices. If that experience could be generalized, then there is some hope that the situation could be remedied. However, many resettlers are reluctant to go down the path of high-input, high-yield agriculture. They fear that inadequate rains or some other factor would render the more expensive inputs uneconomic.

Increases of Actual Cost over Projected Costs Is Minimal

The original resettlement and environment program costs were estimated at $10.4 million. Most of this was for resettlement. Costs increased only six percent, to $11 million. This works out to just over $1,000 per resettler, or $6,000 per family.

Compensation Is Inappropriate and Misunderstood

Compensation for loss of house was the principal form of compensation. This consisted of cash compensation for the lost house and construction of a quasipermanent, two-room core house. There were three compensation rates for houses according to their materials. If people were not home when the assessment was made, or if they disagreed with the calculation, the compensation rate was renegotiated until mutually satisfactory. Less than one percent of resettlers protested at the time. A core house was provided for each household as a means of temporary shelter, while the household was expected to use its compensation money and other assets to construct its replacement house. CEB provided core houses composed of two rooms, made of cement with a zinc roof. Houseplots measured between 17 by 20, and 30 by 30, meters.

CEB took until 1990, three years after resettlement, to pay the final installments of house compensation. The result was that resettlers had to build houses with their own resources, and some sold off assets to do so. CEB house construction techniques were poor, so houses were much less durable than they could have been.[5] CEB never intended them to be permanent, but the resettlers assumed they would be. Therefore, resettlers have faced additional expenses when the core houses were no longer usable. Resettlers were not well informed about the house compensation and replacement process and were cut off from food and other assistance with insufficient explanation. While CEB justified cutting assistance as avoiding resettler dependence, the result is that resettlers had inadequate information and therefore had to make speculative decisions that often were poor choices in hindsight.

Households were given $222 additional compensation for moving voodoo items, conducting religious ceremonies at the time of departure from the old village and arrival in the new village, and for the general inconvenience of having to relocate. It was a significant help to households with meager houses, as the total compensation varied between $370 and $5,555 among the interviewed households.

The compensation was received and spent many years ago. Indicative information suggests that the largest part was used for consumption. Many resettlers had already built their replacement houses before they received all or any of their compensation, so not much compensation was spent on houses. The payment of compensation shortly preceded the general decline in the Togo economy, so many households spent their compensation on subsistence. As farmers were pressured toward more intensive agriculture, some used their money for improved inputs. A few households started businesses, paid for apprenticeships, and found other income-generating uses for the money.

Land compensation was handled in a manner typical for Africa. Resettlers did not receive direct compensation for land: they were not legally the owners of the land they lost. Land belongs to the state, but traditionally it is distributed to households by village chiefs according to need. CEB attempted to move most of the resettlers into previously uninhabited or relatively sparsely populated areas where there were few users of the land. CEB allocated land houseplots and generally indicated which areas farmers could clear for farming. Resettlers chose individual house and farm plots. The problem with this strategy is that it did not allocate sufficient lands for future farming that would use extensive, rotating agriculture and would have to sustain a growing population.

The land had to be cleared for planting. Togolese farmers clear lands annually to plant a yam crop, as yams require fresh soil. At first CEB planned to clear the land for them, but in the spirit of participation, CEB decided to have farmers clear their own fields and to pay them per hectare cleared. Later, CEB decided not to pay the farmers anything for fear of seeing the settlers spend this amount of money on purposes other than agricultural production. Instead, these funds were allocated to an agricultural program.

The land by the river was relatively moist, and tree crops had an important economic function in the old villages. During times of need, farmers could sell their tree products for supplementary income. CEB originally planned to pay cash compensation for the trees but changed its policy and offered replacement seedlings instead. Resettlers rejected seedlings as a substitute (except for 3,000 teak seedlings for shade trees) for several reasons. The arid and rocky soils would not support tree crops. They feared that they would have to pay taxes to harvest the grown trees, or that host community farmers would interpret tree-planting as asserting ownership rights. The issue of compensation for lost trees other than teak has been left outstanding for ten years. This has been a point of contention with the resettlers and is one of the ways in which they say they are worse off since the dam.

With Inadequate Support for Crop Intensification, Resettlers Lose Income

The resettlement plan's only income restoration strategy was to relocate the affected people into a sparsely populated area where it was assumed that resettlers would recreate their former agricultural economy. Land intensification may have been implied, but did not come about because of the lack of support services to facilitate such a transition. The breakdown of government services during the economic crisis is at least partly responsible for the failure to implement more fully an intensification strategy. The only supplemental income strategy was to develop the reservoir fishery, but the Government of Togo vacillated on whether to permit fishing in the reservoir.

Resettlement impacts are highly village and resettler specific. Nonetheless, certain general effects can be ascertained.

The most widespread effect has been on farming incomes. Like total incomes, some farm incomes have increased and others have decreased. Slightly more than half the resettlers interviewed said that their crop incomes had decreased, mainly because of declining yields. Because their area in production is limited to the amount of land they can work, these farmers are trapped in a downward spiral unless they can find a landowner who is willing to give them access to land that is more productive. On the other hand, crop incomes increased for a number of resettlers. One way or another they got ahead of the curve, started earning a surplus, were able to hire agricultural labor, and brought more land into production. Often they were the farmers who could afford improved inputs and thus achieved increased yields, further contributing to their income and surplus, and fueling the growth cycle. In several ways the rich are getting richer and the poor are getting poorer.

Income from trees has undoubtedly decreased. Land in the old village was already marginal for tree crops, and the new land is generally too arid and rocky for oil palm and other lost economic trees. Only a few resettlers have been able to grow economic trees successfully. The only form of tree income that appeared to be increasing is that from charcoal production, a sign more of desperation than opportunity.

Livestock income probably decreased as well. The resettlers' insecure land tenure discouraged livestock raising. Nonetheless, some resettlers had made satisfactory arrangements with neighboring hosts and reported increasing livestock herds. Again, resettlement effects varied according to individual situations.

The Government of Togo has had an inconsistent policy toward developing the reservoir for fishing. For the first four years, 1987–91, fishing in the reservoir was prohibited by the Office of the President. During a brief political liberalization, the ban was lifted and fishing grew rapidly, particularly by skilled fishermen from Mali and Ghana. Following disputes between outside fishermen and locals, and the general lack of a regulatory framework governing fishing, local authorities decided to reimpose the ban, but no regulations were formulated. Given the legal vacuum, locals have been discouraged from fishing.

Nonfarm income plays a very minor role among resettler sources of income, but it appears to be increasing. The main nonfarm income source is petty trading. There certainly are greater opportunities for marketing with the new road network. There are very limited services and no manufacturing in the area. People whose farm incomes decline have few if any alternatives and are more or less trapped.

What can be asserted with reasonable confidence is that resettlers have lower incomes than before resettlement. Increasing land scarcity is putting pressure on farm incomes throughout the area, and although this may not have been caused by resettlement, resettlement probably accelerated the process.

Project Changes in Social Services and Infrastructure Have Mixed Results

Resettlers used to obtain water from the Mono River, although at distances up to seven kilometers. Although CEB's initial provision of pumped water gave people access to water within one kilometer, with the breakdown of most of these pumps resettlers now have a worse water supply situation than before the dam. People have to go up to 15 kilometers to find water. Others have hand-dug open wells up to seven meters deep, but the water is brackish and unreliable. The situation is close to intolerable.

The transportation situation has definitely improved since before the dam. Previously there was not even a good bridge over the river, and people on the left bank of the Mono (northeast of the river) were isolated. The project constructed about 100 kilometers of roads. Now there is a good laterite road system to all the villages and an asphalt road much of the way from Nangbeto to Atakpamé. Access to markets, educational and health facilities, and so on is greatly improved. Although resettlers in the resettlement zone are now 20 to 30 kilometers farther from the main north-south highway in Togo, the improved quality of access more than compensates.

The education situation definitely improved. CEB built or rehabilitated ten primary schools. Although the healthcare facility is much better, it is short of supplies and staff. Drugs are no longer free or subsidized, thus putting them out of the reach of many. This is related to the general reduction of government services and subsidies in Togo.

Resettlers Are Disappointed and Distrustful

Resettlers have a fairly critical perspective on the resettlement experience. Because they are still disputing compensation and because a follow-on project is now planned, resettlers have an incentive to exaggerate the shortcomings of all aspects of resettlement. It is difficult to differentiate between what they say and what they really think.

Many resettlers are upset with the compensation, but that may be because of misunderstandings and later developments. Resettlers expected their core houses to be permanent and are angry that these houses have deteriorated. They felt they did not receive adequate land compensation. They did not understand CEB's policy changes on clearing farm plots and on tree cutting. These misunderstandings led to mistrust and resettler dissatisfaction, justified or not. This is unfortunate, as CEB had built up good will with resettlers before relocation.

Resettlers believe that some aspects of their lives have improved while others have worsened. Overall, most people seem unhappy. However, most people in Togo have suffered a real decline in living standards during the 1990s. Accordingly, the following remarks are limited to aspects specific to their resettlement.

Overall, resettlers are negative about their change in housing. Many have smaller houses than before (but sometimes built of better materials), and even those who now have larger houses often had smaller houses for several years before they recovered and could afford to build new houses. Views on community infrastructure and services are mixed. An inadequate water supply is one of their most frequent complaints. The majority say that health care is worse now. That is largely because of increased costs, which reduces their access. Resettlers are much more positive about changes in education. Schools are generally closer to their homes now, and secondary education is within reach. Resettlers reported that they value education more now; they have a greater appreciation of its contribution. Transportation has improved so much that some resettlers say they would like to have stayed in their old villages if only good access roads had been built to those villages.

One of the most frequent complaints was the resettlers' sense of abandonment, that CEB dropped them near uncompensated host villages, and left them to fend for themselves. Compared with their expectations,

- Their CEB houses deteriorated more rapidly.
- Water systems were less productive, more overused, broke down more often, and cost more to repair.

- Tree crops were never compensated and seedlings did poorly in the different environment.
- Hosts became increasingly less welcoming, and land tenure and access became an increasingly thorny issue.
- Subsidies on drugs, agricultural inputs, and so on were reduced or eliminated, placing these goods out of the reach of most.
- Life overall became much more difficult.

CEB and the dam are blamed for much of this.

Country Commitment Is Good on the Short-Term Inputs but Lack a Long-Term Perspective

Although CEB was slow to hire staff for resettlement and to develop the resettlement plan and was not as explicit as it could have been, CEB and the Government of Togo agencies have in general done most of the right things. For example, they selected, on the basis of land capability and land use maps, areas generally suitable for resettlement. They let the people to be displaced decide on where they want to go, and with which "chiefs." They put the onus of rebuilding houses in the communities on the people, but provided food aid as an incentive to build them. They assisted people with transport to the new villages; provided key services, including water supply, schools, and a dispensary; and involved key ministries in the resettlement process. They made no attempt to introduce radical changes in technology, especially agriculture, letting farmers retain their personal initiative. They also promoted formation of village development committees so that the communities can discuss problems and decide things for themselves.

However, there was a failure to make the transition from relocation assistance to rehabilitation, and the government agencies that were entrusted to provide follow-up did not do so, except for cotton marketing and water-pump repair (for a few years). Lacking clear specification of what that follow-up would entail, it is not possible to determine what actions were not implemented, nor is it possible to determine whose lapse led to the lack of follow-up.

Now CEB and the Bank are committed to remedying the situation of Nangbeto resettlers as part of the new Adjarala project. (The Adjarala Hydroelectric Project, downstream of Nangbeto on the Mono River, will include a component to further assist resettlers at Nangbeto, as the Bank and CEB have realized that problems have emerged.) For that remedial work to be effective, CEB needs to become fully aware of the predicament of the Nangbeto resettlers. So far CEB continues to maintain that "the resettlers are not doing that badly" and they "do not think the resettlers' situation has worsened." However, repairing broken pumps or even compensating for lost trees ten years late will not solve the fundamental problems of insecure land tenure; insufficient land (or inputs); and declining per capita production, yields, and incomes. Further, CEB cannot solve problems that are prevalent throughout the country and need to be addressed as part of the country's development strategy and the Bank's country assistance strategy.

Participation During Planning is Good, but Tensions Build during Implementation

Resettlement planning and implementation were relatively participatory, especially by the standards of the time. Each village formed a committee to supervise its resettlement, and committee members were paid. CEB held many public meetings, and both resettlers and host communities were consulted on and involved in resettlement planning. Affected people participated in designing the program, constructing the replacement houses, and selecting village sites and household plots within villages. Locations of new villages and farms changed because of people's inputs.

NGOs could not work in Togo under the military regime that held power at the time of Nangbeto's construction and the resettlement program. NGOs are just beginning to develop in Togo. So far none are working in the Nangbeto area, but there certainly is need for their services.

Relations with host communities are complicated and explain much of what happened, but they are far from universally negative. Many resettlers have relatives among the host communities. Many said they were able to borrow land from host people for no more than a cola after harvest. Given that the host communities were not offered any incentives to accept resettlers, and did not receive water systems they believe they were promised, they have been hospitable. That they use resettler village water systems is understandable considering the expectations they had of receiving their own systems. Through March 1987, when relocation to the resettlement zones was completed, there was no conflict. Tensions developed only over time. Hosts, too, are suffering land shortages, because of in-migration and resettlers: they are only trying to protect their interests.

Conclusions

Resettlement at Nangbeto raises some serious questions about the limits of responsibilities and how to evaluate such a project. At what point should income restoration be measured; how many years after relocation? If an entire economy, or region, is declining, what is an appropriate income restoration target in this context? If some villages prosper and others do not, or some households do well but others in the same village do not, what are the implications for judging resettlement performance? If the project's implementing agency lives up to its agreements, but those agreements are inadequate, who is responsible for the poor outcomes?

The compensation process was satisfactory overall; the main shortcoming regarded lost trees. CEB's offer of seedlings was inappropriate considering that the areas to which the resettlers were moving were unsuitable for oil palm. This raises the question of how to compensate people for an asset that cannot be replaced.

The relocation process was well planned and implemented. The sites were well chosen, the process was generally participatory (and worked better where it was), the disturbance was minimal, and in many ways the process was a model. The entire problem was what did not come next. Nangbeto is a case study in resettlement without rehabilitation. There was no income restoration strategy beyond recreating the previous farm economy, nothing done for the host communities, no resolution of the land tenure question, no baseline surveys or monitoring, no clear delegation of responsibility for ongoing services, no follow-up, and no way to really know what was happening to resettlers. Resettlement and rehabilitation effectively ended with relocation, final compensation payments, and cessation of food assistance.

Despite compensation and relocation being generally well handled, there was frustration due to poor communication, confusion, and misunderstanding during the resettlement process. CEB inventoried trees, prepared to pay compensation, offered seedlings, and then dropped the matter. Resettlers thought that CEB would clear the land for them, then that they would be paid for clearing new land. Finally they did the work but were not paid. They thought CEB was replacing their old houses, and that the CEB houses were meant to be permanent, not temporary. The compensation payments dragged on for years. The food assistance was for an indefinite period, and then cut off without warning. CEB maintained the pumps for years, but then stopped. Fishing was prohibited, then permitted, and now lies somewhere in between. The net effect of this vacillation is that resettlers have a sense of distrust or even betrayal.

While the agricultural decline due to population pressure and insecure land tenure was not exclusively the fault of the project, certainly more could have been done to avert its worst effects, especially as these problems were foreseen from the outset. Basically, everyone abdicated responsibility and let the problem unfold.[6]

Many of these problems would have unfolded eventually regardless of what actions were taken. People displaced by Nangbeto cannot be sheltered from making the shift from extensive to intensive agriculture. However, they can be assisted during this transition. They desperately need affordable credit and agricultural technician services—but then so does much of the country. CEB is wary of creating a privileged class of resettlers. However, the Bank's stated policy of restoring pre-project incomes in an environment where most incomes have declined would do just that, protect resettlers from declines affecting most other people. This suggests the need to clarify the Bank's resettlement policy in situations where incomes are declining. Presumably the Bank's policy of do no harm should be interpreted to mean that resettlers should be no worse off in relative terms (relative to nearby, similar, unaffected people), not in absolute terms.

Notes

1. Butcher, Memorandum, D. Butcher, consultant, to J.F. Bauer, WAPEG, April 23, 1987, p. 5, makes numerous specific recommendations regarding the handover, p. 6.
2. Although the dam, reservoir, and resettlement areas are all completely within Togo, hydro-power development on the Mono River is shared between Togo and Benin, which jointly shared power before the Nangbeto Project through the binational power company CEB.
3. The lower appraisal estimate might be because the decision to create a two-kilometer buffer zone around the reservoir for malaria prevention had not yet been made. The number of affected villages in the SAR, 34, was accurate.
4. Cotton is exclusively a cash crop, while most of the other cash crops are also partly consumed. There are very limited markets for some crops because transport costs are too high relative to volume and value. If the value of home consumption is imputed, then cotton would not be the most valuable crop for most farmers.
5. Zinc roofs are considered an indicator of relative prosperity by local standards. Most of the inundated houses had thatch roofs and simple mud walls, not mud-cement block walls. There-fore, the resettlers assumed that the replacement houses were meant to be permanent since they appeared to be more durable than their existing houses. In Togo, permanent is relative, as many houses need to be substantially rebuilt after about ten years.
6. Part of the problem in ascertaining the situation is that the project files relevant to resettlement virtually disappear after May 1987, as a result very little is known about what monitoring, surveys, services, Bank supervision, and other follow-up was undertaken.

8

Lessons Learned
and Recommendations

The cases in this book show that if countries do not have both the capacity and the commitment to handle involuntary resettlement well, they should not embark on a large dam project. For years, the infrastructure and human sides of the projects were utterly disconnected in most instances. That is now changing, as more countries voice their commitment to better handling of resettlement. However, the better signal of that commitment would be putting stronger monitoring and evaluation in place.

The best signal will be when governments treat resettlement not as a problem but as an opportunity. One key element in this is to mix land-based and diversified strategies, not just to restore people's incomes but to improve them. A second is to get outside the traditional project cycle and instruments. That means looking for income-generating opportunities well in advance of resettlement and continuing to assess how the resettlers are faring after the dam and resettlement are complete. It also means going beyond the project's finance to tap other sources. The third key element is to work with NGOs, private players, the government agencies, and external donors—to give development a chance.

Capacity and Commitment Are Both Essential

Public sector agencies, for the most part, are limited in their capacity to handle resettlement. In most of the study's cases, public sector agencies mishandled or ignored resettlement. Frequently the public agencies have a technical mandate, unrelated to resettlement. In India and Indonesia, the irrigation department was initially responsible for resettlement; in Thailand, Brazil, China, and Togo, it was the power generating authority. In addition, obtaining the cooperation of other public agencies that are needed to make resettlement a success (for example, agricultural extension, health, and education) can be difficult.

Genuine country commitment to doing resettlement well is the key to success. In China, where the commitment to restore settlers' incomes was a clear mandate, the resettlement succeeded even in remote areas like Yantan. In India, the strongest pressure the Bank could bring to bear did not influence resettlement success in the face of the absence of government commitment. Bland assurances conveniently forgotten guarantee failure. Above all, monitoring and evaluation have to be an integral part of planning and implementation—not a World Bank—inspired exercise that enters and exits with the Bank's presence. The borrowers' undisguised indifference must give way to their recognizing these tools as the essential basis for improved management.

Governments are becoming more committed to good resettlement. In two of the cases here, borrowers exceeded World Bank standards. There naturally are many levels of commitment. Sometimes there is commitment at higher, more policy-oriented levels but relatively less at the resettlement officer level, where the resettlement posting is sometimes viewed as an undesirable two year career step. At other times dedicated individuals in the field are frustrated by indifference at higher levels, which robs them of the resources and other needs to perform effectively. In Brazil, although the implementing agency intended to provide the infrastructure and services resettlers needed, the federal government did not or could not allocate the funds needed to do so. This led to delays that further increased costs. In Indonesia, implementation proceeded without knowledge of the large number of affected villagers who refused to move because local governments were not responsible for reporting on their migration. Although central government's commitment was questionable in any case, the lack of follow-up at the local level aggravated the situation. At Nangbeto, too, responsibilities could not be successfully transferred as planned to local government services.

Improving incomes is too big a challenge for implementing agencies alone. Except in China—where decades of experience with a command economy, allocating jobs, and planning for incomes provided the necessary institutional capacity and political will—government agencies and bureaucracies lack the flexibility and grassroots experience to design income-generating options well suited to resettler capabilities and needs. NGOs should be called on to make a much greater contribution. The private sector can also be drawn in. Looking ahead, governments should solicit cooperation and useful inputs from the earliest stage. Successful resettlement requires innovative approaches using a wide range of public, private, community, and institutional partnerships.

In all circumstances, adequate resource allocations are essential. That environment must outlast the construction period. Government commitments on the budget side—an area where imaginative ideas are needed if resettlement is to work—have to be maintained. In Brazil, Togo, India, and Indonesia, relocation preparations and resettlement activities lagged because too few resources had been dedicated to them. In Thailand, by contrast, ample resources enabled the implementing agency to satisfy resettlers.

The Devil Is in the Details

Planning for Economic Rehabilitation, the Weakest Part of Resettlement Plans, Needs to Improve

Economic rehabilitation of resettlers is the weakest aspect of resettlement planning. This was clearly the case in Togo, where rehabilitation was not even an afterthought. So, resettlers' income and living conditions deteriorated for years without the implementing agency even realizing it. Nor were the strategies based on transmigration assumptions viable for many resettlers at Karnataka, Itaparica, and Kedung Ombo. The planners either failed to address the operating constraints adequately or avoided the issue until it was too late to implement a good strategy. They were forced into second-best solutions or, worse, they developed no solutions.

Intelligent planning does not necessarily imply microplanning. A general structure of plausible income opportunities is enough to establish a basis for budgeting and initiating interactive implementation with the resettlers in a regional context, after which the real lessons about feasible and popular options can be documented and fed back into the cycle.

Relying on the regional economy to take up the slack is risky, especially where overall economic prospects are uncertain. In none of the cases did the authorities specifically rely on regional economic growth to ensure income restoration, but the absence of regional growth was a complicating factor in the Itaparica area of Brazil, in some of the affected areas in Indonesia, and in India and Togo. Planners have to present plans with land and nonland options, flexible models, and fall-back positions in case the regional economy cannot quickly absorb the displacees. Planners should aim for a viable package, adequately managed and funded, that by itself can establish the conditions for restoring full employment—even when the economy is stagnant.

Results, Not Plans, Are the Appropriate Touchstone for Quality Management

Although intelligent planning is a prerequisite to sound implementation, excessive reliance on "paper plans" is dangerous. Reality almost always differs from plans. When it came time to move in Indonesia, despite surveys of villager desires before planning the Kedung Ombo resettlement, far fewer people were willing to enter the transmigration program than had originally said they would go. In China, plans estimated that larger numbers of people could find farm-related employment than proved to be the case. In both cases, adjustments had to be made.

This is the downside of the otherwise positive progress with planning. Although better planning usually means better implementation, this assumption has not held up for involuntary resettlement. As a subsidiary operation, resettlement continues to receive inadequate attention during implementation. In none of the six cases did implementation follow plans, either because implementation failed to keep up to the timetable, or because plans made incorrect assumptions about resettler needs and desires. Countries that monitored results and had sufficient flexibility to alter plans when warranted generally did the best. China, which altered its land-based income restoration strategy when farm employment did not reach high enough levels, is the best example of this. Results, not plans, are thus the appropriate touchstone for quality management. In the cases examined, planning received disproportionate attention in comparison with results.

The earlier Bank review of resettlement recognized this growing disconnect between improved planning and sluggish implementation, and emphasized action and results on the ground—the same message sent by this current study. The point of attack for portfolio improvement has clearly shifted from policy and planning to procedures and practice.

Compensation Must Be Adequate and Timely

Land compensation, the most difficult part of the dam-related compensation package to get right, needs to be handled early, but even this does not guarantee success. Pak Mun's original land compensation rates proved too low—as land prices increased when the reservoir rose, and successive compensation increases only pushed land prices higher. When large numbers of resettlers take unrestricted cash packages and compete for a limited land pool, land prices spiral beyond all reasonable budget limits. China does this job properly by counting heads, identifying opportunities for land-based employment, then broadening the search to take up the excess. In Brazil, if land compensation based on nearby resettlement had been considered earlier, the analysis could have led to something other than the high-cost, high-risk irrigation schemes that were negotiated.

Offering resettlers land-for-land is an option for income restoration but not the only one. In none of the six cases did the land-for-land strategy alone lead to growth. Pursuing land-for-land policies where the circumstances are unfavorable will produce unsatisfactory results, as they did at Itaparica. Governments have had difficulty finding ways to compensate for losses of cultivable land by providing comparable farm holdings nearby. The alternatives have been equally disappointing. Governments had difficulty establishing, with or without donor support, other bases for productive employment. In retrospect, the two tasks are among the most challenging in development: big dam sites usually eliminate the most productive farming systems in the neighborhood, while the people in the flooded valleys have few skills and less motivation to shift to other activities. While land-for-land should be given due consideration and appropriate analysis, it should not be adopted regardless of costs.

Cash options need to be on the list. Inevitably, the dam will result in less land of lower quality being available for resettlers around the reservoir. Since resettlers generally wish to remain close to their original homes, a cash option provides alternatives unavailable from the land-only option, for resettlers to pursue other income-generating options or to improve their homes. In Thailand, recipients used cash compensation to make financial reallocations among household members, so that children could buy houses or land, get better education, or get ahead in an occupation. In Togo, the voodoo compensation was a significant help to the poorest resettlers, and compensation in general helped resettlers get by when the economy collapsed.

The most enterprising resettlers do best on their own and reduce the economic and management burden of the resettlement operation. Tied-cash options—with installment payments, joint accounts, and specialized training programs to steer excess families away from the land—are underused instruments. The Indian authorities have tried these methods, but so far without much success. Clearly, they will not work everywhere, but they have good potential.

Emphasis Should Shift from Income Restoration to Income Improvement

Interruptions to the previous lifestyle along the river—while they can and should be mitigated—are usually inevitable and characteristic of a modernizing economy. They do not mean the resettlement program has failed. Conversely, fairness and equity require that the disruption in the quality of life of affected communities not only be compensated but also be managed to community and individual advantage. The emphasis should shift from restoring income levels, which can suggest recovery to—but stagnation at—predam lifestyles, to improving income levels, which brings the displacees into the developmental process along with the project's primary beneficiaries. Restoration must be treated as the minimal acceptable outcome, even though for some programs that target will be difficult to achieve.

In planning for land-based as well as non-land-based occupations, it is essential to be realistic about the resource base, the activities it can support, and especially, the skills and traditions of the displacees. In none of the cases were initial plans correct about adequacy of the resource base or the desires of the displacees. Itaparica is perhaps the saddest case, demonstrating the results of inadequate understanding about the resource base and the traditions of displacees. Even if the irrigation infrastructure had been put into place on the timetable needed, technical assistance would have been required to give subsistence dryland farmers the skills they needed for the land-intensive irrigated farming they were expected to adopt. At Itaparica, the hope was to settle the families that chose the rural option on small lots irrigated by sprinklers and dependent on unfamiliar, high-input and high-output farming practices. Results on other irrigation schemes in the São Francisco River valley suggest that well over half these families will eventually ask to be replaced.

The income-generating schemes have to be diverse. They aided resettlement success in China, Indonesia, and Thailand. They provided income supplementation in Togo and India to families that otherwise would have had their incomes fall. However, in China, income diversification was a conscious policy of the resettlement authorities. Marketing channels must be identified and, if possible, ensured before venturing into new crops, products, or services—or significant expansions of existing activities. An income-generating scheme is only as good as its weakest link.

Most of the successful resettlement experiences in the study were either not land based or were very land intensive (for example, mushrooms and fish cages). Almost all the self-resettled households moved toward non-land-based economies. Recreating existing production systems, while sounding culturally superior, is often not feasible for dam resettlement. However, because many families are likely to opt initially for maintaining their previous lifestyle, alternatives must be researched thoroughly, organized well, and presented and discussed to the families' satisfaction.

Diversification after displacement—especially behind big dams—almost always implies greater risks, harder work, and loosening of family and community bonds. Despite their desire to remain close to their original homes, many families had to accept migration—temporary or permanent—of family members to supplement incomes. This is a more desirable alternative, however, than the situation in Brazil, where families remain on their new farms to receive title to them, but in the meantime teenagers and young adults are idle.

Adequate Financial and Material Support Are Key to Providing Effective Social Infrastructure and Services

A big issue is dealing with local administrations, in jurisdictions much larger than the resettlement community, that are disinclined or unable to continue to favor resettlers with special services. Those administrative units have larger constituencies to serve, including many other poor families and sometimes including families suffering from structural adjustment and other Bank-supported programs that do not offer compensation or safety nets.

Nevertheless, the social infrastructure created under the program has to be accompanied by adequate staff and supplies. Schools and clinics without teachers, nurses, textbooks, and medicines are useless.

Participation by Resettlers was Surprisingly High but Should Still Be Improved

Participation rates were surprisingly high: good to begin with in some programs and improving in others. Yet the countries should focus even more on strengthening local organizations. The effect of aggressive interventions by representative self-help organizations can be astonishing. In the three cases with strong involvement—Kedung Ombo, Pak Mun, and Itaparica—these organizations ultimately achieved policy changes that influenced the outcomes. In China, the strong participation of local government provided the program with the flexibility needed to adapt its income restoration strategy. This is where China excels: the village leadership does just that—leads the way in employment creation—and the leaders that fail are removed. Pólo's contribution at Itaparica is another example.

A little-noticed success story emerged, at Kedung Ombo, under the worst conditions for participatory behavior. There, villagers surprised all observers by defining the rules and organizing the cultivation of the drawdown area—an asset that had not been realized—and helped cushion the negative effects of the dam. By contrast, the failure of Indian villagers to organize to recover incomes, in particular their inability in Maharashtra to press for the completion of the promised irrigation canals, stands as a sad example of missed opportunity.

Nongovernment Organizations Should Be Encouraged to Participate More but Should also Avoid Being Intransigent

NGOs are logical choices for doing baseline socioeconomic surveys, organizing resettler participation, and intervening at the grassroots level. The main problem in the projects studied was not using NGOs enough. Frustration with advocacy should not prevent countries from valuing NGOs as useful sources of information or having productive relationships with NGOs. The resettlement programs in this study suffered from too little voluntary, constructive grassroots activity by NGOs. Although the success stories, China and Thailand, succeeded without it, the other programs could have benefited substantially. However, NGOs should take care to avoid creating a confrontational or abusive relationship with resettlement agencies where accommodation may yet succeed.

Relocation Should Be Treated as a Development Opportunity

The Number of People Displaced Should Be Reduced.

Given the complexity of resettlement and the unimpressive track record for both land and nonland strategies, the first principle must be to reduce the number of people affected, until financial and economic returns argue otherwise. Work on minimizing displacement—one of the pillars of present policy (but hardly evident in this study)—will also show that an analysis of alternatives has been done and that planning is much more upstream and looking at the sector and regional context of the infrastructure proposal.

Compensation of Land for Land Should Be the Starting Point

Countries should dismiss the demand that they choose between land-for-land compensation or no dam, as some NGOs have proposed. The demand is unrealistic. The proper approach is to explore an offer of cultivable land as the most attractive of the possible options, where technical viability, profitability, and the aspirations of the displaced have all been considered in assessing priorities and determining a least-cost budget. Land-for-land should be considered first, but the challenge for most resettlement projects is to develop other options before the land runs out.

Some recent experiences in India have shown that there is still plenty of room for acquiring additional land for distribution through marketplace mechanisms: the supply may be far less static than is commonly assumed. The potential of the land-for-land solution has rarely been fully tested. However, behind many big dams the percentage of displaced families that can be resettled on viable rainfed farms is usually small.

Compensation Should Mix Land-Based and Diversified Strategies

Countries should offer irrigated lots in the command areas (for irrigation projects) and elsewhere support land-intensive activities and traditional dryland cropping. They should also shift to diversification activities (supported by training) and use tied-compensation packages, joint accounts, and tranching payments to promote them. Experience with these options in the study projects has been no more impressive than with resettlement in rainfed areas, and the benefits have been equally elusive. That means putting the best development planners to this task, along with the best resettlement experts. Resettlement must not be seen as an inconvenient add-on but as integral to the project. The emerging concept of resettlement as a development opportunity rather than a burdensome obligation is a step in the right direction. China understands this; the other five countries do not.

Incomes and Living Standards Should Be Improved

Countries should shift the emphasis from restoration to improvement of income and living standards, opening the way for those displacees who are motivated and capable of moving from their valleys to take a new place in the regional or national economy—as an integral part of the project's developmental objectives. The design of the infrastructure project must not only provide water, power, and other conventional benefits below the dam but also be part of a regional development plan shaped to support the affected families above the dam. Enough benefits should be captured to justify the local social disruption and to help establish sustainable, progressive employment and incomes for the displaced. The aged, infirm, and unmotivated may not welcome the opportunity to "modernize," and should not be forced into it. However, the resettlement strategy as a whole should reflect more ambitious aspirations.

What does "restoration" mean if the regional economy is deteriorating (Nangbeto)? When should "improvements" be expected in remote valleys (Yantan)? Clearer specification of objectives, alternatives, and the time-horizon are required for planning, monitoring, and evaluation. Many issues remain unresolved on this point:

- What is adequate restoration if the entire region is booming or, conversely, is deteriorating?
- What percentage of resettlers can be expected (or permitted) to fail?
- What percentage of farmers can still be below the threshold if the average has already moved above it?
- If immediate restoration is impossible under any practical scenario, as appears to be the case, what is an acceptable time horizon?
- Do short-term fixes, such as the monthly supplement paid at Itaparica, ever count?
- Does a resettlement program succeed if the plans do not work but incomes are lifted anyway, even up to the level of nonaffected families, by coincidental developments in the regional economy?

The study suggests, however, that too much concern for standards to measure the restoration of incomes may give the wrong signals about the purpose of involuntary resettlement, at least when associated with big dams. In most instances, the upheaval attending relocation should be managed as a development opportunity and funded accordingly. While restoration is an appropriate short-term objective, improvement of the productivity, living standards, and lifestyles of the displacees is as valid a long-term objective of the project as the improvements planned for the project's primary beneficiaries.

Countries Need to Go Beyond the Traditional Project Cycle and Instruments

Where stand-alone resettlement projects are not feasible, countries need other instruments inside and outside the conventional investment lending program to influence upstream and downstream activities essential to resettlement success. On the upstream side are training and testing new strategies. Downstream, other devices may be necessary. Since the monitoring and evaluation of resettlement impacts and resettler incomes tend to disappear when the Bank exits the project, continuing Bank involvement in supervision through the resettler rehabilitation phase would support improved monitoring. Further financing may also be necessary. Retrofitting older projects that failed to accommodate all the displaced can be expensive, as with Karnataka.

Governments Should Work with the Private Sector

The private sector is expected to take the lead in dam construction in the future. This will increase the pressure on government to intensify upstream activities that ensure resettlement components are adequately prepared and specified. Postconstruction responsibilities also have to be defined and specified in the contracts. Failure to assign responsibilities and accountability on actions essential to resettlement could have terrible consequences. Private sector projects raise new legal issues, for example, the limits to invoking eminent domain for private profit.

Summary

Countries need to explore all available options, and to mobilize the energies of all their development partners, to achieve better resettlement results. This applies especially to projects involving substantial movement of people, the loss of present occupations, and the complicated task of generating new jobs and livelihoods. Big dams are the quintessential example of where such an "incomes" approach should be used. Many resettlement components in other projects, by contrast, will continue to be primarily concerned with reestablishing houses and community infrastructure after urban, highway, and other dislocations—maintaining jobs rather than creating new ones. This "shelter" approach may not need radical redesign, for this study's investigations show that in all six countries' compensation for lost houses and construction of new ones has been reasonably well handled.

The total flooding of prime valley land is the only category of involuntary displacement where cultivable land in quantities large enough to accommodate the displacees usually is not available, except through long-distance relocation, expensive irrigation, or both. All resettlement planning for postproject employment must offer choices among feasible alternatives implying the need for flexibility. Preference should be given to land-based resettlement strategies for people dislocated from agricultural settings. If suitable land is not available, non-land-based strategies built around opportunities for employment or self-employment may be used.

Above all, displacees must be beneficiaries of the project. Merely aiming to restore standards of living and lifestyles common to isolated river valleys can be a dead-end development strategy. The opportunity must be taken to establish new and dynamic sources of sustainable growth. In nonreservoir cases, that impulse may be less compelling, because communities are usually not so deeply disrupted. The recommendation applies especially to big dams because they involve major social dislocations and thus require special arrangements. Many families are likely to be apprehensive about "dynamic growth," and their legitimate concerns can be addressed only by excellent preparation of the most cost-effective alternatives with the families' full participation.

Index